D1119896

ESSENTIAL REFERENCE SERVICES FOR TODAY'S SCHOOL MEDIA SPECIALISTS

ESSENTIAL REFERENCE SERVICES FOR TODAY'S SCHOOL MEDIA SPECIALISTS

Second Edition

Scott Lanning and John Bryner

Libraries Unlimited
An Imprint of ABC-CLIO, LLC

Santa Barbara, California • Denver, Colorado • Oxford, England

Library of Congress Cataloging-in-Publication Data

Lanning, Scott.
Essential reference services for today's school media specialists / Scott Lanning and John Bryner. — 2nd ed.
p. cm.
Includes bibliographical references and index.
ISBN 978–1–59158–883–2 (acid-free paper)
1. School libraries—Reference services. 2. School libraries—Reference services—United States. I. Bryner, John. II. Title.
Z675.S3L265 2010
025.5'2778—dc22 2009039375

14 13 12 11 10 1 2 3 4 5

This book is also available on the World Wide Web as an eBook.
Visit www.abc-clio.com for details.

ABC-CLIO, LLC
130 Cremona Drive, P.O. Box 1911
Santa Barbara, California 93116-1911

This book is printed on acid-free paper ∞

Manufactured in the United States of America

For my wife, Maria, who made everything possible, again.

Scott Lanning

For my children, who inspire me to be better.

John Bryner

Contents

List of Figures

Preface

Reference librarianship has changed dramatically in the last 20 years. The whole process of finding information has undergone a fundamental shift. Print resources have given way to various incarnations of electronic resources bringing us to today's Web resources. Yet books have not been replaced. Everything is not on the Web and not all Web resources are free. Progress has not simplified the job of reference librarians. We need to be aware of many more sources and many more ways of finding information than ever before.

The role of the reference librarian has changed as well. We are on the front lines of information literacy. Each reference encounter is an informal opportunity to teach information literacy skills. Each library instruction session is a formal opportunity to teach these essential information literacy skills.

The role of the school library media specialist has also changed dramatically. The library/media center is not just a study hall with books and a stern librarian making sure no one is talking. The school media specialist is an integral part of the school. Today's school media specialist is an equal partner in reaching the school's educational goals, an active participant in teaching, a colleague who shares special expertise with other teachers to improve instruction throughout the school, a promoter of media center resources and services, an advocate of the importance of information literacy to students and teachers alike, and a reference librarian.

This book is aimed at those people who are interested in becoming school media specialist and media specialist who want to improve their reference skills. It shows these essential skills in the context of today's information literacy standards and the new, unique role that library/media specialists play in their schools. The material in this book is designed to give you a solid foundation in all aspects of providing reference services to your students and teachers from a practical point of view.

The book focuses on three main areas: core reference skills, electronic resources and leadership skills. Core reference skills includes a discussion of information and information literacy in Chapters 1 and 2. Chapters 3 through 5 examine evaluation of resources, print resources and the reference interview.

Chapters 6 through 9 comprise the section on electronic resources. Chapter 6 focuses on library catalogs while Chapters 7 and 8 discuss how to search electronic resources and the Web. Chapter 9 talks about creating your own Web resources.

Leadership skills comprise the last four chapters. Chapter 10 discusses your role in teaching the core curriculum. Chapter 11 talks about selecting materials for the reference collection that will meet curricular and learning goals. Chapter 12 examines the importance of evaluating reference services. Chapter 13 ends the book with a discussion of the leadership role you need to take to promote reference services and information literacy and how you can help your teachers and school in reaching their curricular goals.

It was a wonderful learning experience for us to put this book together. We hope you enjoy reading it, and we also hope that you will learn something new and valuable from this book that will help you provide exceptional reference services to your students and teachers in today's rapidly changing and exciting library environment.

Chapter 1

Information

In this chapter we will discuss what information is and where it comes from. We will examine how information moves from producer to user and how you and your students gain access to it. Finally, we will look at the value of information as it ages.

WHAT IS INFORMATION?

What is information? Here's a good definition from the *McGraw-Hill Dictionary of Scientific & Technical Terms* ("Information" 1994).

> *Data which has been recorded, classified, organized, related, or interpreted within a framework so that meaning emerges.*

We need to know what information is because we are learning how to find and use it for ourselves and our students. Keeping our definition in mind, let's look at a few examples.

- 00001000
- 120741
- 29028
- 231

Is this information?

No, it's data. It has no framework, no context from which it can be interpreted. If you knew the first item was in binary, you would be able to interpret it as the number 8. If we rewrote the second item as 12/07/41, you would know it's a date and that might be all the framework you need to know it is the date of the attack on Pearl Harbor. If we told you the third item was a mountain, then you would know that 29,028´ is the height of Mount Everest (Janssen 2008). Finally, if we added an mph after 231, we have given you more data and maybe enough of a framework for you to guess that 231 mph is the highest recorded wind speed in the U.S. ("Wind Speed (Surface)" 2007).

How many of those did you know?

What we were looking at in our example was data, because it had no organization, classification, or framework to give it meaning. Data can be called raw information. Once we process the data, it becomes information. That relationship is an important one. Data needs to be interpreted before it can become information. Data by itself does not have much value, but information does.

We now have an information scale with two steps. Data is the lowest step. Once we give it meaning, we step up to information. There is a third and final step on our information scale, which we'll mention briefly: knowledge. Knowledge happens when a person takes information and organizes it to help answer a specific question, solve a problem, or make a presentation or report of some kind. Knowledge is a personal and internal reorganization of information with a goal in mind. When you share your knowledge by giving a speech or writing a paper, you present your audience with information that they must process and assimilate into their world view to create knowledge for themselves. Data, information, and knowledge are the steps on the information scale. Each successive term has more weight or value than the preceding term.

WHERE DOES INFORMATION COME FROM?

Let's work through an example:

A research scientist is working in the rainforests of South America. She has been there many years. She spends her time studying the plants, alone, and hasn't had any human contact since she's been there. She's found new species and recorded information on the growing conditions, life cycle, and chemical properties of each of these plants. She hopes that this information will lead to a better understanding of rainforest ecology, a stronger interest in preserving it, and, most remarkably, new drugs to fight diseases.

Has she generated information? She has been collecting data. She has the knowledge to interpret that data, to give it a framework, and create information for herself. However, she has not been generating information for anyone else. She needs to do something else before we can really say that.

Let's suppose now that our researcher leaves the rainforest after ten long years. She is very excited. She has notebooks full of data that she wants to share. She gives that data a context from which others can understand it by writing an article and preparing a conference presentation. She gets her article published and speaks at conferences all over the world. Now she is sharing the information that she has generated.

This is the "something else" she needed to do: share her information with the world in a formal manner. Why is this important? Her work is now cataloged and classified by others. It's available. It's accessible. Anyone can learn from it and librarians can guide others who are interested in it to that information.

Where else does information come from? Does information come from world events? TV news? A local paper? What about a film, or a novel? Are these sources valid ways to get information?

Sure! We're bombarded by information every day. When a friend tells you what just happened in his history class, that's information. We rarely receive data. When we do, we usually say, "what's this?" or "where did this come from?" or ask some other clarifying question to help us understand—to convert the data to information.

HOW IS INFORMATION RECORDED, CLASSIFIED, AND ORGANIZED?

Our definition says that data has to be recorded, classified, etc., in order to be called information. So where does this happen and who does it? The recording part is easy—it's written down, videotaped, photographed, tape recorded, printed, painted, or any other way you can think of to "record" the information.

Our rainforest botanist needs to find a journal to publish her research, which will record and share her knowledge with others. Fortunately for her, the publishing industry's output is vast. Our rainforest botanist will be able to find a journal with the same subject interests as hers in which to publish her articles. *Ulrich's Periodicals Directory* (2007) lists 55 pages of botany journals. Our researcher could also check the listings under ecology or forestry for even more possible journals. Though it might not seem like it, you could say that the publishing industry's output is organized by subject due to how it publishes to meet the interests of readers.

Classifying and organizing information is an interesting step in the process. Institutions like libraries try to organize information by using classification systems such as Dewey Decimal and Library of Congress. The federal government tries to classify its publications by issuing agency using the Superintendent of Documents Classification System.

WHERE DOES INFORMATION GET INTERPRETED AND ANALYZED?

Our researcher recorded, classified, analyzed, and interpreted her data and wrote an article about it. She's part of the whole process. Now that she has published her article, everybody else gets to be part of the process, too. Information is interpreted and analyzed by anyone using it, and that includes your reading of this document right now! You are the one who decides whether or not information has any value for you. A specific piece of information may not mean anything to one person, but may be of the utmost importance to you.

HOW DOES INFORMATION GET TO YOU?

To answer that question, let's look at the diagram below.

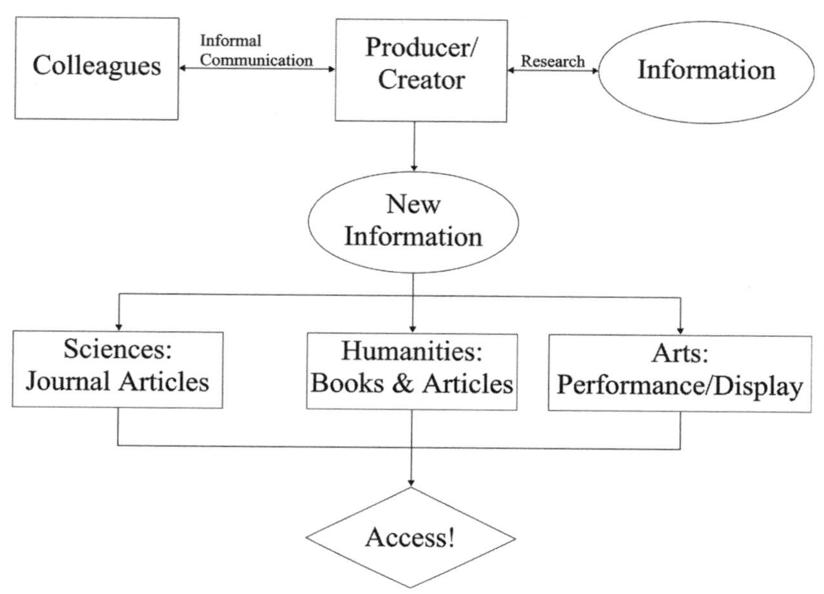

Figure 1.1. The Flow of Information

The Producers/Creators Must Get Their Work "Published"

Not everyone has to get their work published in a magazine for it to be "published." If you do a report on earnings projections for your company, you wouldn't expect Time magazine to publish it. However, your report is shown at the big meeting, so people know that it exists, and it becomes part of the company's files—their store of information. Storage for future retrieval is analogous to what we do with materials in the library.

There are many reasons producers/creators would want to share their work with the world: they want to get tenure, they want to make the world a better place, and they want personal recognition. For whatever reason, producers of new information "publish." "Publish" is in quotes, because there are many ways to publish your work. If you paint a masterpiece, you don't get it published in a journal. Instead, it is displayed at a gallery. If you make a movie, you show it. If you create a dance, you perform it. Once it has been published in some form, it can be stored and made available to others for their review or enjoyment.

"Publishing" takes many forms—all of which can be cataloged and made available in our school libraries. Let's look at the ones I've listed in Figure 1.1.

Journals

Journals are important to all academic disciplines, but, due to their nature, they are more important to the sciences. Can you think of some reasons? What if there weren't any journals. The best you could do were books that were published annually. The books are very good publications, representing their various disciplines very well. Would you find the latest research in one of these books? You would find the latest research *published*, but *not* the latest research. Books take a long time to put together: selecting and editing articles, printing and binding the pages, distributing and selling the books. By the time the latest book reaches your hands, the information could be a few years old, and then you have to wait another year before you get any more information!

The problem in the sciences is that there are new discoveries made every day, and yesterday's news is of diminishing value. The publication schedule of journals helps solve this problem of currency. Journals are published anywhere from four times a year to once a week. The hotter the discipline—the more research being done in an area—the more publications there will be, and the more likely that there will be a weekly publication. While articles for journals still need to be selected and edited, and the journals need to be printed and bound in some fashion, the whole process is more streamlined, more responsive, and serves the needs of sciences very well.

Add to this the fact that many journals are currently made available in an electronic environment, and now you and your students can keyword search those journals for articles and print them out immediately.

Books

Like journals, books are important to every discipline. Books can summarize the "current" state of knowledge in a discipline, and synthesize it into a cohesive whole. Books give their authors more room to operate, to make their case, to illuminate themes and support their conclusions. The humanities are still a book-oriented discipline. That's not to say they don't have their journals, but unlike the sciences, the latest and greatest thinking on a topic might not be what was printed yesterday, but what was printed 10 years ago. An old idea that's a good idea will find its way into books.

Performances and Displays

If you are a choreographer, you can write a journal article or write a book about dance, but you are more likely to choreograph and stage a dance. Performance and display of works by visual and performing artists is a way to get their work "published." If these performances are recorded in some way—an exhibition catalog, video tape, or a review—they can be used in a library.

Other Media?

What other media can one get "published?" CD-ROMs and DVDs hold vast quantities of information and allow for interactive learning and entertainment.

The Web is a tremendous medium for publication. Aside from basic production costs including equipment and time, there are no printing or distribution costs, and it supports a variety of media, including print, graphics, and video. Traditional print publishers have started to publish many of their titles electronically as well as in print. Electronic forms of publishing are definitely here to stay.

ACCESS

Why all this talk about publishing? How does this fit with a discussion about libraries? Good questions. Let's say our rainforest researcher returns home with her notebooks full of wonderful information and she never publishes any of it. Only a very few people would know about her research and only a few of them would have learned about it firsthand. The others would have learned about it second- or thirdhand. Not only would a very few people actually know about her research, but only a select few people would also have access to her research, and all that valuable, important information would never reach its full audience where it could do the most good. Publishing provides access to information, and access is what libraries are all about!

When you move on to other chapters in this book, keep this idea of access in mind and see how it fits with school library resources. The whole idea of a school media center is to facilitate easy access of published information to students and teachers so they can examine it and create their own knowledge—one of the keys to lifelong learning.

THE AGING OF INFORMATION

Let's end this chapter with a question: Does information have a life cycle? We've seen that it has a beginning with a producer/creator or an event. Its middle years are publication, analysis, synthesis, and use. But does it have an end?

There may not be a good answer to that question. Let's look at an example and see.

It's ten years later. Our rainforest researcher is still around. Her original work is no longer new, but many other researchers have used her work as a starting point for their own. Her article gets cited in many other articles. Her work is still clearly of value. It has matured and is in the prime of its life, so to speak.

Ten more years pass. Our researcher's work is not cited much anymore. New research is no longer based on her work, but on the work of people who followed her. Her information has grown old.

In the next ten years, no one cites her work. Has her information come to the end of its life cycle? Even in this carefully controlled example, the answer is only *probably*. One hundred years after she published her first article, it may again be of interest to someone researching the history of rainforest science.

However, that interest will not be enough to fully revive our researcher's work. Information grows old, but it ages at different rates depending on the discipline. A book about the Civil War that is ten years old may represent the state of the art in thinking about the war. However, a ten year old book about treatments for diseases may be dangerously out of date.

Information gets added to, built upon, updated, and replaced. An outlandish theory one year may become a proven fact the next. Information is constantly changing and will continue to do so. Of that, we can be certain. We must be aware of this change and understand how it impacts the value of information so that we can help our students find the best information available.

Some information weathers the onslaught of time better than others. Shakespeare has been going strong for 400 years. Most information does not have this kind of staying power. It not only grows old; it fades away, completing its life cycle.

Chapter 2

Information Literacy

In this chapter we discuss the principles of information literacy. We look at the Information Power standards and the Big6 Skills that can be used to teach the standards. We talk about critical thinking, the *Common Sense*[3], and why this is all important to you and your students.

WHAT IS INFORMATION LITERACY?

Information literacy is the ability to recognize when information is needed, locate, evaluate, and use information efficiently, effectively, and ethically to become an independent, lifelong learner.

That is our working definition. It is pieced together from the definition stated in "Presidential Committee on Information Literacy: Final Report" that is available at the American Library Association Web site (1989) and from the numerous definitions listed by Webber and Johnston (2006). These definitions were remarkably close to each other with only a few minor differences: some may mention ethics and some not, some may mention efficient and some not. This basic agreement on what constitutes information literacy is good to see. Information literacy is an important concept and by agreeing about what it means we can get on to becoming information literate ourselves, and teaching our students and colleagues to do the same.

Let's examine the definition more closely. The first part of the definition states that to be information literate, we need to recognize an information need. In other words, we need to know that we need to know something. We need to be aware that we have a question to be answered. In addition, we need to know how to formulate good, clear questions that focus on getting our information needs answered.

Next, with our research question in mind, we need to be able to locate the information. Where can we find the answer to our question? Is it in a book in the library or in a database we can access from the library, or can we find it on the Web?

Once we locate the information, we need to evaluate whether or not it is useful to us. Does it answer our question partially or fully, and is it good, reliable, accurate information?

Finally, we need to be able to make use of the information—to apply it to our original need. We have to be able to do all this efficiently and effectively without wasting time, getting to the good information quickly. We must be ethical in our use of the information we found by giving credit to the authors of the information through citations.

HOW DO WE AND OUR STUDENTS BECOME INFORMATION LITERATE?

If we can understand these basic steps of information literacy, and teach them to our students, we will all be rewarded by becoming independent, lifelong learners. Does this mean the ultimate goal of information literacy is to eliminate the need for reference librarians? No! We will be constantly teaching information literacy skills, and just because someone understands the research process does not mean they know what sources to use or terms to search. Reference librarians will still have plenty to do. The real goal of a school media specialist is to help students become more information literate so they can learn well in school and in life. "Information literacy . . . is the keystone of lifelong learning" (*Information Power* 1998). It will help students in school, adults at work, and anyone who has a question that needs an answer.

"Creating a foundation for lifelong learning is at the heart of the school library media program" (*Information Power* 1998). Luckily, there are some well defined standards and procedures that have been designed to help us in that great endeavor.

THE *INFORMATION POWER* INFORMATION LITERACY STANDARDS

The Information Literacy Standards for Student Learning from *Information Power: Building Partnerships for Learning* (1998) are designed to give school library media personnel and teachers guidance in teaching information literacy to their students. These standards are powerful tools and are well established within our community.

Here are the first three of the nine standards. These three relate well to finding information that may be part of a curriculum goal and a student assignment.

- Information Literacy
  - The student who is information literate accesses information efficiently and effectively.
  - The student who is information literate evaluates information critically and competently.
  - The student who is information literate uses information accurately and creatively.

The second three standards are targeted at helping students become more independent in their learning. These standards relate well to the concept of lifelong learning even outside the classroom. They describe a person's choosing to learn about topics on their own, appreciating creative works of all kinds and even generating new knowledge.

- Independent Learning
  - The student who is an independent learner is information literate and pursues information related to personal interests.
  - The student who is an independent learner is information literate and appreciates literature and other creative expressions of information.
  - The student who is an independent learner is information literate and strives for excellence in information seeking and knowledge generation.

Building on the first six standards, the last three focus on a literate person's responsibilities and possible contributions to others in a democratic society.

- Social Responsibility
  - The student who contributes positively to the learning community and to society is information literate and recognizes the importance of information to a democratic society.
  - The student who contributes positively to the learning community and to society is information literate and practices ethical behavior in regard to information and information technology.
  - The student who contributes positively to the learning community and to society is information literate and participates effectively in groups to pursue and generate information.

From *Information Power: Building Partnerships for Learning* by American Association of School Librarians and Association for Educational Communications and Technology, 1998. Reprinted with permission of the American Association of School Librarians, a division of the American Library Association. See www.ala.org.

For each of the information literacy standards *Information Power* lists a few indicators each with three levels of proficiency: "basic," "proficient," and "exemplary." All of this information can get a little confusing; first there are the nine standards, then several indicators that describe the standards, then levels of proficiency that describe the indicators that are describing the standards. Wow!

School media specialist should keep in mind, however, that it is the nine standards that they are required to teach to their students. The indicators and proficiency levels are suggestions meant to help you know if your students are meeting those nine basic standards. To see the indicators and proficiencies, you will need to refer to the book (*Information Power* 1998).

While this is a lot of information to learn and digest, the *Information Power* student information literacy standards are meant to be the basis for the school library media program at any school. They deal with integrating information literacy skills into the curriculum and building an information literate future for all of your students.

The American Association of School Librarians (AASL) recently introduced new standards. Let's take a brief look at these.

STANDARDS FOR THE 21ST-CENTURY LEARNER

Standards for the 21st-Century Learner (2007) are the newest standards for student learning developed by AASL. Based on a set of common beliefs, like the importance of reading, technology skills, and school libraries/media centers, the standards are (Reprinted with permission of the American Association of School Librarians, a division of the American Library Association. See www.ala.org.):

Learners use skills, resources, and tools to

1. Inquire, think critically, and gain knowledge
2. Draw conclusions, make informed decisions, apply knowledge to new situations, and create new knowledge
3. Share knowledge and participate ethically and productively as members of our democratic society
4. Pursue personal and aesthetic growth

Each standard is further subdivided into four areas. Skills are the first and most obvious. This section lists the set of skills and abilities students should have to meet the standard. Dispositions in Action is the second area. This is the most difficult of the four to understand. It is defined as the "ongoing beliefs and attitudes that guide thinking and intellectual behavior that can be measured through actions taken." Dispositions are then a set of actions that increase inquiry and knowledge, share results, and pursue continued personal growth. Responsibilities are about finding, using, and sharing information responsibly, ethically, and legally. Finally, Self-Assessment Strategies are ways that students can assess their own success in each of the four standards.

These new standards are similar to the *Information Power* standards, touching on each of its three main areas. So, were the 21st-Century standards designed to replaces *Information Power*? According to AASL's FAQ (2008) the answer is no. The 21st-Century standards are designed around the need for multiple literacies such as technical, visual, and digital.

There are other models of information literacy out there. Another very popular model is the Big6™ Skills. Let's take a look at what the Big6 brings to the table.

THE BIG6 SKILLS

Listed below are the Big6 Skills (Eisenberg and Berkowitz 2000). Much like the *Information Power* standards, each skill is subdivided, specifically into two sub-skills.

1. Task Definition
   - 1.1 Define the problem
   - 1.2 Identify information needed

2. Information Seeking Strategies
   2.1 Determine all possible sources
   2.2 Select the best sources
3. Location and Access
   3.1 Locate sources
   3.2 Find information within sources
4. Use of Information
   4.1 Engage (e.g. read, hear, view)
   4.2 Extract relevant information
5. Synthesis
   5.1 Organize information from multiple sources
   5.2 Present the result
6. Evaluation
   6.1 Judge the result (effectiveness)
   6.2 Judge the process (efficiency)

Many states have included information literacy standards in their core curriculum (Murray 2003). The Big6 is one popular method of teaching these standards. For example, the public schools in Utah use the Big6 Skills, which are part of their core curriculum, as their guide to teaching students information literacy ("Library Media").

A BRIEF ANALYSIS OF INFORMATION POWER, 21ST-CENTURY, AND BIG6 SKILLS

All of these programs are intended for K-12 audiences. They talk about the importance of integrating information literacy into the curriculum and encourage school librarians to get all the teachers at their schools involved. One major difference between *Information Power* and the Big6 is that the first two are standards-based, and the last one is skills-based.

Information Power and 21st-Century are standards-based. A "standard," according to *Webster's 2nd* (1953), is "in general, a definite level . . . viewed as that which is proper and adequate for a given purpose." A standard is a baseline that is considered so important that all students should meet it. The fundamental goal then of a school media specialist is to help all students meet these standards and therefore encourage a more literate society.

The Big6, on the other hand, is skills-based. It is designed to help you apply the broad goals of *Information Power* and 21st-Century to an individual assignment or information problem. If the Information Power and 21st-Century standards are the information literacy standards we want all of our students to have, the Big6 is one way to help us teach some of those standards to our students.

The Big6 states that it is a problem-solving strategy (Eisenberg and Berkowitz 2000). Clearly, it is a step by step approach to an information problem. It is very process oriented: first do this, and then do this, and so on. It is skills based. It breaks down the process of finding and using information into steps that students can learn now, and as their skills improve, they will develop a deeper understanding of the steps and information literacy.

Let's take a look at critical thinking, a foundation for *Information Power*, 21st-Century, and the Big6, and also for our own Common Sense^3.

CRITICAL THINKING

> Critical Thinking is . . .
> Logical thinking based on sound evidence. A critical thinker can accurately and fairly explain a point of view that he or she may not agree with (McBrien 1997).

Logical thinking includes analyzing, comparing, contrasting, generalizing, problem solving, investigating, experimenting, and creating. Critical thinking "is integral to lifelong learning and the capacity to deal effectively with a world of accelerating change (Critical Thinking 1997)." That definition should sound rather familiar.

Is the similarity in the definitions of critical thinking and information literacy the reason we should be talking about critical thinking? Yes, but there's more to it than that. The Big6 acknowledges critical thinking as important, for one thing. It's been around for a very long time, for another. Our last definition of critical thinking sounds a lot like why librarians say information literacy is important.

Critical thinking, regardless of what we call it, is what we try to teach. We try to teach our students how to learn.

Let's look next at the Common Sense^3. It tries to simplify what we've looked at so far while adding a theoretical basis. It may help you understand what all this information literacy stuff has been about.

THE COMMON SENSE^3

In the old days, which were neither good nor bad, just different, we had the concept of library literacy. The definition was simple: library literacy was learning how to use the library and its resources. But that was when libraries did not have any electronic information sources. Times have changed.

We have replaced the idea of library literacy with the concept of information literacy. After all, the library of today looks very different from the library of the old days. In fact, even the term library is old fashioned. It implies a room filled with dusty books, not the media centers of today with their rich variety of media and wealth of electronic information. The thinking goes that because things have changed so much for the better we need something bigger and better than library literacy. We need to talk about information literacy.

We've looked at the definition of information literacy. It is indeed quite broad. In fact, it may be too broad. We may be better off splitting up the idea of information literacy into its component parts to aid in our understanding. The three parts are all literacies themselves, but more narrowly defined. The three literacies are: library literacy, information literacy, and knowledge literacy.

Library literacy is still a valid concept with a definition and scope that are easy to understand. We define library literacy as being able to use a library and its resources efficiently and effectively, and being able to critically evaluate the information source. It is primarily taught in the library/media center.

Information literacy is defined broadly as being able to evaluate information itself, not the information source. Evaluation of information can be taught either in the library or the classroom.

The last of our three is knowledge literacy. Knowledge literacy is the new concept added to the picture. It is based on the idea of knowledge management, which is a popular concept in the business world. The definition of knowledge literacy is being able to integrate and apply information. There is no library/media center component to this definition. It is beyond the scope of both library and information literacy because it is about the application of information, the creation of knowledge. It can only be taught in the classroom where the student is applying this skill.

The new model is called The Common Sense^3, or *CS*^{3}, because there is nothing new or revolutionary about it.

- The Common Sense^3
  - Acquire
  - Evaluate
  - Apply

Acquire is recognizing the need for information, identifying the nature of the information needed, and finding relevant information. This matches up nicely with library literacy.

Evaluate is determining whether the information gathered is relevant to the information need, evaluating the quality of the information retrieved, the process used to find the information, and the final product. This is information literacy.

Apply is integrating, using, and producing information. It is expanding your personal knowledge base, your wisdom. This is knowledge literacy.

The three also form steps. You need to know how to acquire information before you can evaluate it. You need to evaluate the information you've retrieved before you can apply it. It is also easier to learn how to acquire information than it is to learn how to evaluate it or learn how to apply it.

We learned of another three-step scale in the first chapter of this book: that of data, information, and knowledge. Is there an analogy here? According to our definition of data, libraries house information—data that has been processed and given meaning. However, the library is where we do our research, our data gathering. So library literacy is the process of collecting data. Information literacy is then evaluating the data that we found to see if it is useful in the context of our information need—to see if it is indeed information to us. Finally, knowledge literacy is assimilating and applying the information we found to our need. This is *CS*^{3} in action.

Can a fourth grader reach the third step—knowledge literacy—and learn how to apply information?

Yes, there are levels of understanding. A fourth grader can learn how to apply information. In fact, students are applying information at even earlier grades. However, a fourth grader cannot be expected to have the same level of understanding of the application of knowledge as someone with a PhD. You cannot expect a fourth grader to be able to construct and execute a complex database search; however, they are perfectly capable of pointing and clicking their way through a Web site.

The *CS*^{3} is a simplified way for you to think about information literacy, the skills you need to teach and the standards you need to meet. We hope it will help you understand the Big6 and the AASL standards and your role in teaching them.

WHY ALL THIS TALK ABOUT INFORMATION LITERACY?

What has this got to do with school reference services? These are good questions. Reference services at any K-12 school incorporate library instruction, and the relationship between library instruction and information literacy is obvious. But how does information literacy impact the reference transaction? In order to answer this question, picture yourself at the desk in the media center. A student approaches you with a question. The actual question itself is irrelevant. Think, instead, about the philosophy you will use to answer the question. The philosophy, you may ask? Yes. What is your guiding principle? What are you trying to do with your reference service? If you say, "answer questions correctly," you are only partially right, but you have missed the point of the AASL standards and the Big6 skills.

Your job is to teach your students how to find the answers for themselves, and teach them so well that they will choose to go on finding their own answers. Every encounter with a student is an opportunity to teach them how to use library resources and thus teach them information literacy skills. This is why information literacy is important to all reference services.

Chapter 3

Evaluating Reference Sources

In this chapter, we will discuss the five elements of evaluation: relevance, purpose, validity, format, and arrangement. We will also discuss why it is important for you and your students to know how to evaluate resources. Finally, we will provide an evaluation checklist to make the process a little easier.

DOES MEDIUM MATTER?

As a school media specialist, you are responsible for collecting materials in all kinds of media: Web resources, CDs, CD-ROMs, video tapes, DVDs, cassette tapes, slides, 16 mm films, photographs, maps, models, film strips, and, yes, even books. Well, you may not collect all the media listed here. Formats come and go, but information resources will always need to be evaluated to see if they will be a worthwhile addition to your collection or a good answer to a question. In this chapter we'll learn about some basic guidelines you can use when choosing reference and other materials for the library and you and your students can use to evaluate information for both school projects and personal use.

First, do you think each medium should be evaluated with its own set of guidelines? Different media can enable different presentations of information, and different methods of accessing that information. This may require some special consideration, but the general guidelines we will present below still apply whether the item is a book or an electronic resource. Let's start by addressing the importance of knowing how to evaluate resources.

THE FIVE ELEMENTS OF EVALUATION

One obvious reason we need to know how to evaluate information is to be able to select the best materials we can afford for our collections. But there is another reason that is just as important. As school media specialists, we need to know how to teach our students to select and evaluate the best information to answer their needs. This is a big part of our role in producing information literate students, especially in a world where such vast amounts of both good and bad information is becoming so easily accessible.

The elements of evaluation outlined below can be used by you when considering a resource for purchase or by your students when they are considering information for use in classroom or personal projects.

Our five elements of evaluation are

- Relevance
- Purpose (includes type, scope, and style)
- Validity
- Format
- Arrangement

When you read other material or take library classes, you will very likely encounter variations on these basic elements. The names may be slightly different. There may be more or fewer of them, but the purpose is the same: to give you and your students a means to evaluate resources. These evaluation guidelines are very important. You must know them and know how to apply them if you want to provide the best materials for your students and be able to both use and teach those resources to help your students find the information they are looking for.

With that said, let's move on to the first evaluation guideline: relevance.

RELEVANCE

We're starting with relevance because it is the easiest and the most basic of the guidelines. Students can find a lot of information quickly and once they do, they need to ask, is it relevant? Does it help me answer my information need? As a media center specialist, does it fill a need in my collection? Will my students use it? Whatever survives this first cut should relate to the topic, question, or need being researched. From here, a more in-depth analysis can proceed.

PURPOSE

The purpose of the resource encompasses the type of resource it is, its style and its scope. There are three basic types of resources: primary research, primary sources, and secondary sources. These distinctions start to come into play in upper elementary grades. The concepts are so important with the information boom of today that students could certainly be introduced to the ideas even earlier.

Types of Resources

Primary research reports on the results of an original experiment or research project conducted by the authors of the material. The journals you and your fellow teachers read have articles that are primary research. Primary research is often very structured. It will state the hypothesis, the methodology used to test it, the outcomes, and a conclusion.

Primary sources are materials from individuals or time periods that are used to study those individuals or time periods they lived in. If you were studying the Great Depression, then primary sources would be letters, diaries, newspapers, photographs, and other documents produced during that period in history. If you were studying FDR, then a collection of correspondence would be a primary source for information.

A secondary source, on the other hand, is any source that incorporates primary sources or primary research. An encyclopedia article is a good example of a secondary source. There will be no original research in an encyclopedia article. Instead, you will find a synthesis of current thinking. There may be excerpts from a primary source, but the focus of the article will be a commentary on the primary source or its time period.

Scope

Scope is what is or is not covered or included in the resource. Scope consists of the breadth and depth of the information provided in the item. A research article in a journal may be very narrowly focused. Other topics are so broad that the authors have to make decisions about what aspects of the topic to cover and at what level of detail.

Let's look at the Civil War for our example. Our collection consists of four books: *Famous Battles of the Civil War*, *A History of the Civil War*, *Letters Home from the Civil War*, and *Life During the Civil War*. The titles of each book give some indication of scope, but we are going to look more closely at each one.

Famous Battles is only about famous battles. What battles are considered famous and what were the criteria for inclusion? What battles were excluded and why? Those are the obvious questions to ask about the scope for inclusion in the book. There are more, of course, such as what kind of information is given about each battle, and how much information is given?

Our second title is a history. In the preface, it says that the book covers all aspects of the war: political, military, social, and economic. The book is 150 pages long. How much coverage can each topic be given in that amount of space? Will it have as much information about battles and life as our famous battles and life during the war books?

Our third book consists entirely of letters from soldiers. It is arranged chronologically. Will this book give us a broad overview of the political aspects of the conflict? Will it detail battle plans?

Our last book covers what it was like to live during the time of the Civil War. It talks about things like economic conditions, wages, working conditions, what a typical home looked like, how it was furnished at various class levels, and political beliefs of the people as a whole. While it is a good book like the others, it makes no mention of any battles, does not talk about what our political leaders where trying to do, and is not on a personal level like the collection of letters.

These differences between our books come down to scope, the breadth and depth of coverage. How much of the topic of the Civil War did each choose to cover and in how much detail? If you had to choose one of these reference books for your collection, how would scope influence your decision? If you had all these books in your reference collection, would you know the strengths and weaknesses of each and be able to guide students to the most appropriate one? For students, the question of scope is Does the information resource answer my question? Is there too little or too much information, or does it match the scope of my project? If there is a big mismatch between the scope of the resource and the scope of my project, will I be able to extract relevant information to use? This is scope and why it's important.

Style

Style is the author's choice of words in the broadest sense. Style is how the author writes, his tone of voice, his intended audience, his point of view. Style is much more strongly associated with fiction and even informational books than it is with reference materials, but with our broad definition, you can see that style is an important consideration for all library resources. Imagine a dictionary that defines words with circular definitions, or by using at least three more words that you need to look up to understand the definition, or by such vague language that you don't know what the word means after reading the definition. While there isn't much you can do to make a dictionary definition exciting reading, it should be clear and understandable to its intended audience. This is a function of style.

A reference or informational source should present its material in a straightforward, evenhanded manner, but the tone of voice can differ. Most reference materials have a formal, scholarly tone of voice. A few have an informal, conversational tone. Some reference materials and informational sources choose their words and tone to make the material easier for children to follow and understand. While one approach to style is not superior to another, the overall style of a particular resource can be more appropriate for certain audiences while being entirely inappropriate for others.

The intended audience of the material affects its style. A book written for sixth graders will not have the same vocabulary or tone as a book written for college students. What is considered scholarly for a sixth grader is very different from what sounds scholarly to a college student. The style, how the information is conveyed, needs to be appropriate for the intended audience.

Point of view is generally to be avoided in reference material but is the hallmark of fiction and important to nonfiction as well. Point of view is the perspective that the author brings to the material or even imposes on the material. Point of view can range from an evenhanded presentation of all sides of an issue or a presentation of the facts of a research study to blatant propaganda that tries to convince its audience of the rightness of its opinions in the absence of facts. The authors of a reference or informational resource should not be trying to sell you on their opinions but should be presenting the facts as supported by research. A book with a scholarly tone can be selling ocean front property in Arizona. Don't let tone influence your understanding of point of view.

Point of view often leads back to accuracy and authority. If you encounter an article that has a strong point of view, examine who the author is and who published the article. If an author says that smoking tobacco is not addictive, you may discover that the article was published by a tobacco company, an organization that has a vested interest in promoting a specific point of view.

It's very important for students to learn about point of view. Students will often use editorials from newspapers or journals in their reports because they don't understand that an editorial is an opinion piece that may have no supporting evidence. The Web presents even more problems. It's easy for students to scoop up large amounts of information that may look good but that has a strong bias and misrepresented facts. Students need to be able to spot snake oil salesmen.

VALIDITY

While validity seems like it should be a simple and straightforward concept, it has a number of components that interact with each other to build the whole picture of a resource's validity. The components of validity are

- Timeliness
- Accuracy
- Authority

These three components of validity will help you select good resources for students to use in your library, but they are also important ideas for students to understand and use themselves, particularly when evaluating resources. Today there is certainly a lot of accurate information available for students to use on the Web, but it is just as likely that what they find will be inaccurate in some way. Understanding and applying these principles can help them evaluate and choose the best resources.

The components overlap and are dependent on each other. While we need to break accuracy down to get a good grip on it, we also need to keep the whole product in mind. If a reference item is weak in any one of these areas, it's probably a good idea to find a different reference source. Encyclopedias, for example, are often discarded after five years because their information is dated and no longer accurate.

So, how do all the pieces fit and work together? Let's look at timeliness.

Timeliness

Timeliness not only asks how current the information is but also whether that information is based on the latest research. While timeliness is important, it is more important to some disciplines that to others. For some disciplines and topics, like the sciences, the timeliness or currency of the information is of vital importance. New discoveries are happening all the time. Information becomes dated, quickly. For other disciplines, the age of the material is not as important as the quality of the material. If you were writing a paper on Shakespeare, you can find lots of great information that is still valid even though it may be many years old.

Timeliness is easy to ascertain. You check the publication date. Keep in mind the publication process has an effect on timeliness. The newest information in a book published this year may be at least one year old. That article on the latest discovery may have taken four month to get published in a journal. A Web page could be updated on a daily basis.

Aside from the publication date, there is another aspect of timeliness that you need to consider when examining items. It is the publication dates of the references cited. This is important because you can have a book that was published yesterday, but all the works it cites, all the works that its ideas are based on, were published 40 years ago. A work like this cannot be considered to be up to date or current despite its publication date.

Let's say you have two items in your collection that you would like to update. Both of them are 10 years old. The first is a book about dinosaurs. The second is a book about U.S. history. You only have enough money to update one of the items. Which item would you update? How would timeliness effect your decision?

Accuracy

Accuracy is the veracity of the information presented. It was a long-standing fact that Mount Everest was 29,028´ tall. The height of the mountain was taken recently with modern GPS equipment. It is now a fact that Mount Everest is 29,035´ tall (Brunner 2008). Anything that gives the first number is wrong, and therefore, inaccurate. While this is a simple example, it can be difficult to know if the information being presented is correct or not.

One way to check is to compare what two or more resources say about the same thing. If there is agreement, then the source in question measures up. It is a daunting task to evaluate the correctness of a reference source. We often rely on reviews to provide us with this information. We do buy materials without the benefit of reviews. In that case, it wouldn't hurt to spot check the new resource when it arrives. When looking at a magazine article or a Web site, for example, students may run into a similar problem: how do I know this is accurate? The solution is the same: find another resource that says the same thing.

This sounds difficult. It is also why we rely on other aspects of validity to give us some assurance of the accuracy of the information, such as reputation of the author or publisher and publication date. However, students, even younger students, should be taught to use more than one resource. This builds in the comparison of information and should help students uncover inaccurate information.

We've already mentioned looking at the references in an information resource for their timeliness, but references can also be checked to help evaluate accuracy. Which do you think may be more accurate, the 500 page book with a 15 item bibliography or a 200 page book with a 50 item bibliography? You also need to look at the items in the bibliography. If the article you are reading is a research paper, but the items it cites are all from newspapers and news magazines, then you should question the accuracy of the article.

Authority

Authority is who wrote the material and what their qualifications are. Authority is more than the authors' credentials; it is also the references they choose to support their work and the publisher who published it. In classrooms of the past, students depended almost entirely on the texts and other materials that were selected by teachers and librarians and were unconcerned with the authority of an item. But today students need to know how to check the authority of an item, particularly if that item is a Web site.

When it comes to reference books, most are written by PhD's. This can level the playing field. However, look closely at what the author's degree is in and what the book covers. If the author has a PhD in criminal justice, does that qualify her to write a book on psychology?

In large reference sources like encyclopedias, the articles are written by many different people. Is each article signed by the person who wrote it, and what are that person's qualifications? Are all the contributors, the authors of the individual articles, listed somewhere in the resource? Are their credentials listed there as well? What about the authority of an article from Wikipedia that is not signed by an author but has many authors who may or may not be credentialed in the field?

Books and journals often list the credentials of their authors. It is a selling point. Web sites, on the other hand, may not provide any information about the author. Should you trust the information from such a site? What's the difference between a .com, .edu, .gov, and a .org site (commercial, education, government, and nonprofit organization)? Does that necessarily affect the quality of the information? Does the author/sponsor of a Web site or other resource have a political agenda?

What else have the authors written? This is easy to check in commercial databases. You click on the author's name and pull up a list of items by that author in that database. Have these works been well reviewed? Have they been cited by others? It may be a hard to find a review of that material. If you have access to a citation database, you can see if an author has been cited by other authors. Very few of us have access to citation databases because they are expensive. However, databases like Academic Search Premier are now including a "Times Cited In This Database" link that gives you some of the same effect as citation database which is a measure of popularity and impact of an article.

We know that the currency of the references cited effects the overall currency of the item. We know that having appropriate references impacts the item's accuracy. Combine these two and add quality references and you have authority. So what are the cited sources? Where are they from? Do they represent the best thinking? Does the author cite only books or only journals? Are they reputable journals and well-reviewed books? Who published the materials? How many citations are there? Does that seem like a lot or a few given the material?

You need to look at the references because it will help you understand the author's intent, which we already talked about in the section on style. It will also help you understand the currency and quality of thinking that went into the item.

The publisher is another point to consider when evaluating materials. While a publisher is no guarantee of quality or lack thereof, it is worth examining. You are more likely to get a good book, journal, or Web site from a quality publisher than from a lower tier publisher. A publisher with a reputation for publishing quality resources has earned that reputation through careful selection of resources and good reviews received by those resources. They are unlikely to want to jeopardize that reputation by publishing something of questionable quality.

Let's say that you need a book to fill a hole in your reference collection. You have two fliers on your desk for just such a book. One is from Oxford University Press, and the other is self-published by the author. Both books are brand new. There are no reviews, and you need one as soon as possible because an assignment is coming up that will require this material. Which one would you order sight unseen? Both books might be good, but at least with the book from Oxford University Press, you know it won't be bad.

When examining a publisher, look at what else they publish and how it has been reviewed. When examining a journal article, teach your students to check if the articles underwent a peer review process. In a peer review, articles are read by a number of experts in the field who then decide if the article is good enough to be published in their journal. This is an assurance of a certain level of quality. To determine if a journal is peer reviewed, look at the guidelines for submission. This will state how articles are selected. Some electronic resources make it easy to find peer reviewed articles. All you have to do it put a check mark in a box to limit your search to peer reviewed journals only.

The publisher of a Web site can be an individual who wrote and created the whole site, or it can be any organization or group. For some Web sites the organization or publisher behind the site is very clear. Examples are recognizable brand names like Wikipedia and WebMD. For other sites, you may have to look closely at the page to determine who the publisher is. Don't forget to consider the domain the Web site is a part of when thinking about the publisher. A .com can be a site created by anyone or any for-profit business and the quality can vary wildly from nonexistent to wonderful. A .org is frequently a nonprofit organization that may have a very specific point of view on a topic. Our government collects and publishes tons of data, so a .gov site can be raw data for interpretation by others. Finally a .edu can represent a university, its researchers and scholarship, but it may also be a student Web site, so be sure to look closely.

FORMAT

These last two items are really more for you in your role as selector of reference items for the collection. While they have an impact on the students' use and enjoyment of the information resource, they are not necessary for students to know in helping them decided if a resource is a good one for their paper.

Format is the physical presence or form of the item. The information that makes up an encyclopedia, for example, may be in the format of a book, a CD-ROM, or a Web site. Even if you had two dictionaries in book format, the format could be different. A pocket dictionary, for example, may be printed in paperback form with thin pages and no illustrations. A more formal desktop edition of the dictionary could be much larger, with many color illustrations. The information is the same, but the format is different.

Format is not the same as arrangement. They are often confused for each other because the words in general have similar meanings. However, our definitions are very different. Format is physical. It is how the item looks. Arrangement is intellectual. It is how the information is placed and accessed within the item. They are both important to a good resource, but in very different ways.

For now, we'll begin our discussion of format by doing an exercise. Take one volume of two different encyclopedias off the shelf, for example, a volume of *Encyclopedia Americana* and *World Book Encyclopedia*, and compare them to each other. Start by examining the size of each volume—height, width, and depth. Which one is thicker, taller, and deeper?

Now, open each volume and look at how the material is presented on the page. How many columns of text are there? What font is being used? How large is it? How much white space is there? Are there illustrations, pictures, charts, or drawings? Are they in color or black and white? How thick is the paper stock? Is it glossy or dull? How are text and illustrations laid out? Do they work well together?

Do all of these elements help you find/use/read the information? Is the format of one encyclopedia better than another? Is the format better for one age group than another? These are questions of format, the physical presentation of information.

Now take any one of your print encyclopedia volumes and compare it to any CD-ROM or Web-based encyclopedia you have access to. Ask all the same questions of the electronic encyclopedia as you did of the print one. Are all the questions valid for the electronic source? Are there other questions you could ask about the physical presentation of the information that apply only to the electronic version? When you compare the two, which one do you think has the better format?

Is format important to a student doing a paper or project? Perhaps. Illustrations may be particularly important to younger students. Size, portability, and other physical factors may play a role. However, it is the information that students are seeking, and if it is good then these basic issues of format are less important. Of course, you need to keep format in mind when considering materials for purchase.

ARRANGEMENT

Arrangement, as stated above, is the intellectual presentation of the information within the item. This includes all the means provided to access the information. There are many possible arrangements for each type of reference source. Some arrangements work better then others for various types of material. For example, an atlas could arrange its maps by name of country, by population, or by continent. The last choice being the one most atlases use.

Let's use our *Famous Battles of the Civil War*, again, as an example. Our book could arrange the battles geographically, chronologically, by generals involved, or by importance. A print reference source can only arrange the material in the main body of the work—the information at the heart of the book—in one way. An electronic version of this book may offer many ways to move through the information so that you can pick the method that appeals to you the most, like chronological by general. In print sources, tables of contents are created to show that arrangement of information, and to provide a means of jumping into the text. Indexes are created to give points of access to specific pieces of information, and cross references are used to guide you to related information. Our Civil War book could choose to arrange the main body of the work chronologically, and then provide an index that lists generals, locations, companies, casualties, etc.

When looking at a single entry in a reference source or a magazine article, examine the logic behind the presentation of the information. Does it make sense? Will my students be able to use this resource easily? Does the information flow in a logical manner?

Look for the standard features that are included in each entry in a reference resource. Does each article have a history of the topic and a summary of its current state? How about a pronunciation? Is each article signed by an author? Is there a list of further readings or some sort of bibliography? Are these features filler or do they help you use the work and understand the information?

Our book could also have a table of contents, a bibliography, a glossary, an appendix, an introduction, a preface, a list of illustrations, or other features. The main body of the work could divide its materials into chapters with chapter divisions based on theme, geography, chronology, etc. There could be no chapters at all. Instead, the material could be listed by major subject with subdivisions for minor topics or it could just list everything alphabetically.

The arrangement of the information provides points of access. The main body provides one method of access to the information. The table of contents, list of illustrations, indexes, and other lists provide other points of access to the information in the resource. There may be only one index in a book that includes all of the references to the text, or there may be many thematic indexes that pull like items together. For example, our book could have separate indexes for people, places and things, or one index that combines all these ideas into one alphabetical run. All of these elements provide points of access to the information and should be logical and easily usable for yourself and your students.

How many of these print concepts carry over to an electronic reference source? Does it make it easy to use and find the information? What additional features and access points does the electronic resource add? In any format, the arrangement of information in an individual article or a whole reference work should help you find and understand that information. All the pieces should support each other to make the whole a better work.

The World Almanac has an index, something you would expect to find in an almanac. However, the unique thing about the index in *The World Almanac* is that it is at the front of the book, or at least it was until the 2003 edition moved the index to the back of the volume. This illustrates the intellectual nature of arrangement. Someone decided that the book would be better with the index placed at the beginning, and recently someone decided that it would be better with the index in its traditional location at the back. Do you understand why these choices were made? Which do you think is the better placement?

EXAMPLES

As you can see, there are many questions to be asked and many things to be considered when evaluating a resource for quality. The five elements of evaluation overlap and work together to give you and your students a complete picture of the quality of an information resource. The more you evaluate and use resources, the easier it becomes to apply the evaluation guidelines and to judge the quality of resources. Evaluation may seem to be a time consuming process, but the skills involved are certainly expected for both yourself and your students.

Here are a couple of examples to evaluate. A high school student is doing a paper on capital punishment; he finds a Web site he likes, but he is not sure whether it's good enough for his paper. He asks for your help, and you look at his site and notice three things right away. It's a .com, has no author, and lists no publication date. Do you have enough information to make a decision about the possible quality of this site? Would it make a difference if the site had an author and a publication date? What if the site were a .edu or a .org? How would that effect your decision?

Next, you're doing research for an important presentation you have to make to the school district on the value of the school library/media center. You find an article in a database that looks perfect, but when you click on the author's name, you find that this is the only article in the database that she's written. Is that reason enough not to use it? What elements would this article have to include to make you want to use it? Would an extensive and quality bibliography be enough? Or would it need to be published in a respected journal as well? This is why we must learn to evaluate.

EVALUATION CHECKLIST

Use the checklist below to help you or your students evaluate information resources. If you think a resource meets the standard for quality for that guideline, put a check mark in the box; otherwise, leave it blank. Write any notes, pro or con, in the third column. When you're done filling out the form, you should have a clear picture of the quality and usefulness of the resource.

Figure 3.1. Five Elements of Evaluation Checklist

Item being evaluated:		
Relevance	☐ Relevant	
Purpose	☐ Type of resource ☐ Style ☐ Scope	
Validity	☐ Timeliness ☐ Accuracy ☐ Authority	
Format	☐ Medium ☐ Layout ☐ Illustrations	
Arrangement	☐ Logic ☐ Points of access	

Chapter 4

Print Reference Sources

In this chapter we look at the types of reference books that are available and the kinds of information they contain. The types are almanacs, atlases, bibliographies, biographies, dictionaries, directories, and encyclopedias. We end the chapter with a list of representative reference books.

SO WE HAVE BOOKS. WHY WOULD I WANT TO USE ONE?

The primary goal of any school media program is student learning. In fact, the basic focus of school libraries recently shows a definite shift from an emphasis on developing our collections to a strong emphasis on student learning. One way the reference sections in our school libraries could be measured then is by how well the items in that collection end up helping students become more information literate.

With that basic goal in mind, books and other printed materials are still valuable resources as we will show. Taking into account other factors such as price, portability, availability, and accuracy, books will be an important part of our collections for a long time. However, the siren's song of electronic resources tempts our students. Electronic versions of print reference sources are common now, and format seems to be less important to students as they get older. They want to sit down at a computer and do all their work. They don't want to get up and look around the library. They don't realize that the Internet is often not as accurate nor as well organized as many print resources.

TYPES OF REFERENCE BOOKS

There are seven types of reference books that we will examine. They are

- Almanacs, Yearbooks, and Handbooks
- Atlases and Gazetteers (Geographic Sources)
- Bibliographies
- Biographies
- Dictionaries
- Directories
- Encyclopedias

At the end of this chapter is a list of reference books. These books represent examples of types. Some are classics. Others are there to serve as an example. Take a look at all of the books on the list! Most of these books will be easy to find at a school, public, or academic library. If you cannot find a specific book that's on the list, look for something like it. Keep the category of the book in mind. Always think of your students, and how this particular resource might aid them in reaching the school's specific curriculum goals and the student literacy standards in general.

You should look at one type of book at a time. If you look at all the books in the almanac category, you will learn what kind of information is typically found in an almanac. Compare the books within a category to each other. What makes one different from another? How does it fit and not fit within the category? Specifically, you should learn what type of information is contained within each individual book and what types of information is contained within each category of books. You should also think about what questions each book can answer. Which book would you use if you are asked to name the president of Spain? If you can answer what makes a book an almanac, what's in the *Statistical Abstract of the United States* and where would you go to find a list of the seven wonders of the ancient world, then you've got the point of this chapter.

Finally, apply the elements of evaluation from Chapter 2 to the books on the list. What is their format? How does arrangement affect how you find information in the book? Who wrote and published it? What are their credentials? When was it published and how does that affect the accuracy of the information? Does the book cover its topic with great breadth or depth? What information is included and what's excluded? Who is the intended audience? Do my students need this item? This will build your familiarity with evaluation and your knowledge of these reference sources.

ALMANACS, YEARBOOKS, AND HANDBOOKS

School media specialists and all librarians should be very familiar with this interesting group of reference books. The materials in this category have as many unique properties as they have in common. Typically, the entries are short, except for encyclopedia yearbooks. Coverage ranges from very broad to very narrow and publication is frequent, except for handbooks.

Remember when looking at a book from the reference book list to think about what kinds of information are in the book and also what kinds of questions your teachers and students will be able to answer with that book.

Almanacs

Almanacs are wonderful resources full of short entries and statistics with much of the information arranged into tables and lists. Where else can you find the most popular breeds of cats in the same place as postal rates for a five pound package, the population of Turkey, and the American League batting champions?

Almanacs are a staple of the reference collection, though they can be overshadowed by encyclopedias and subject specific resources. There's nothing like an almanac for a quick fact or figure. For example, students might use almanacs to quickly compare facts between countries and update statistics and information from an encyclopedia article.

Almanacs are published yearly to keep their information up to date. Even so, many librarians have spent a lot of time writing in the names of newly elected officials to keep their almanacs current, and to have one source with the latest information.

Almanacs generally have very broad coverage and include both current and historical information.

Yearbooks

Yearbooks differ from almanacs in that they generally have only current information. This can be a very minor distinction. Where do you draw the line between a source that offers current information and one that offers both current information and retrospective information? What category should *Statistical Abstract* or *Almanac of American Politics* be in? It can be difficult to decide if something is an almanac or a yearbook because the definition does not necessarily fit with the way information is presented. There is a lot of gray area between yearbooks and almanacs.

Like almanacs, yearbooks are published yearly and their scope can be broad or narrow. Publishers used to update their encyclopedias by publishing a yearbook each year. One other difference between a yearbook and an almanac is that yearbooks may contain long articles versus the almanac's short entries.

How is *Guinness World Records* different from *The World Almanac* in terms of the sports records listed? Guinness and World Almanac illustrate the basic differences between almanacs and yearbooks. Guinness is interested only in the current information—the current record holder. World Almanac has the current record holder, plus all the winners of the event at all the Olympiads throughout history. It is a difference in scope. Almanacs have some historical information, and yearbooks do not.

Due to the nature of the information contained within both almanacs and yearbooks, you need to purchase them often to keep them up to date. Do you need to keep the superseded editions for historical purposes?

Handbooks

Handbooks are included in this category because of their short entries. That's about where the similarities end. Handbooks try to give a comprehensive overview of a topic in one volume. The topic can be broad like American literature or more narrowly focused like Herman Melville. In any case, the result is a book with breadth and little depth. Handbooks are not published yearly. To state the obvious, if they were, we'd call them yearbooks. The information provided in a handbook is generally not of the kind that needs to be updated on an annual basis.

For example, the *U.S. Government Manual* gives an overview of the functions of the departments of the executive branch. This perspective would make it a handbook. However, names and addresses are included. This is enough to bump it from the handbook subdivision. Names and addresses need to be updated frequently, and the Government Manual does this by publishing on an annual basis.

On the other hand, the Oxford Companions are classic examples of handbooks. They are one volume overviews of a topic with necessarily short entries. There are entries for people, literary works, places, and ideas. The more important the topic of the entry is to the work, the longer the entry will be. Longer entries are often signed or initialed by their authors, and have a short bibliography or list of further readings. These are some examples of the things you should be looking for based on what you learned about evaluation in Chapter 2.

ATLASES AND GAZETTEERS

We are all familiar with road atlases like Rand-McNally's, and most of us have seen world atlases with their detailed maps of geologic and geographic features, but did you know an atlas can show you how we voted in the presidential elections, trace the movements of people and cultures, and diagram a battle plan?

Basically, any information that can be interpreted or presented in a geographic view can be included in an atlas. There are atlases designed with different audiences in mind. *National Geographic World Atlas for Young Explorers* is one such atlas. How does the intended audience affect the style and coverage of this source compared to a standard world atlas?

Gazetteers are the opposites of atlases. They have no maps and no illustrations, but they are concerned with geologic and geographic features. Instead of maps, you get an alphabetical listing of all the features you would find on a map such as cities, rivers, mountain, etc. The information frequently includes location, specifically longitude and latitude, elevation, population, and history of the place name. A gazetteer is a very specialized resource. It won't be nearly as popular as an atlas, but when you need one, you need one.

BIBLIOGRAPHIES

Bibliographies are lists, and not just lists of books, but of any media. Traditional, print bibliographies once ruled the roost as a research tool. Their importance has diminished greatly since the advent of electronic resources, and they are frequently overlooked, although they are still important to serious students, but mostly in an academic library. However, that is a narrow definition of bibliographies.

Let's say that you are thinking of joining a book club that a friend is in. Your friend gives you a list of the books she has already read. Is that list a bibliography by our definition? Bibliographies are usually held together by a theme. They are not a random list. The book club's selections make a list, and a bibliography is a list. However, the items on the list also represent the personal tastes of the book club. That's the theme that holds the list together.

When you look at the materials in a bibliography, the theme or purpose of the publication should be clear. *Children's Catalog* lists books and magazines for kids from preschool to sixth grade, and is arranged by Dewey Decimal number so you can find books by subject. *Children's Catalog* also has another feature that is common in bibliographies: annotations. Annotations can provide a short summary of the material, like an abstract. However, they differ from abstracts in that they offer not only a summary of the text, but also a critical judgment of the material. The annotations in *Children's Catalog* are excerpted reviews from other sources.

Bibliographies often have clever arrangements of the information in the main body of the work and a wealth of indexes. When you look at the bibliographies on the list, pay special attention to those features. Look at the kinds of information given for each entry. Is there an excerpt from a book review or a citation to one? Did the compiler of the bibliography write critical annotations for each of the items listed?

This brings us to the next point about bibliographies. They can strive to be comprehensive listings or selective. The subject they focus on can be broad or narrow. They can include only available materials, materials that are still in print and/or easy to find, or all materials including out of print materials that may be very rare. They can limit themselves to books, films, videos, journals articles, CD's, or include all kinds of material. Their time frame can be only the output of the past year, or the past 100 years, or all time. Finally, some are updated frequently while others will never be published again. *American Reference Books Annual*, also known as *ARBA*, is a bibliography of reference books and is published annually. If you read the introduction in *ARBA*, you learn that its purpose is "to provide comprehensive coverage of English-language reference books published in the United States and Canada during a single year (*American Reference Book Annual* 2008)." This tells us its scope and more specifically the method used to select materials for inclusion. That's important to know for a bibliography. If you don't want to buy the book, you can subscribe to the Web site (http://www.arbaonline.com). How does the information in this source differ from what you are given in *Best Books for Children*? Do you think the purpose of these two publications is the same or different?

This all gets a little confusing, so let's look at an example. Let's start with a library historian. This historian wants to put together the definitive list of all the books ever published about libraries as an institution. Our historian has already made a number of decisions. He has chosen a narrow subject and is limiting his selection of materials to books only. His time frame on the subject matter is the whole history of libraries, as opposed to covering only the monastic libraries of the middle ages, and he wants more than just the books on library history that are currently in print. He wants all the books ever published on the topic, so he will include very old and rare books, out-of-print books, and current publications. His book will be a comprehensive listing. He will write annotations for each and every entry. The annotations will be a critical evaluation of the books cited. He has no plans to update the list, but hopes that someone in the future will.

So, what has our historian created? A selective bibliography? An annotated bibliography? A comprehensive bibliography? A comprehensive, annotated bibliography? There clearly are many types of bibliographies. When you look at the books on our list, determine what kind of bibliographies they are. What is their scope? How are items selected for inclusion or why are they excluded? How many common traits and unique features do each of the books have?

BIOGRAPHIES

Biographies are very popular items that are commonly read for enjoyment. That is book length biographies. Biographical materials in the reference collection may not be as fun to read, but they provide a wide variety of information, ranging in length from one or two sentences to many pages. Length of entry helps determine which source to use for which information needs.

For example, you are working at the reference desk and it is quite busy. There are a number of people waiting in line for help when a patron asks you when Albert Einstein died. There are literally hundreds of sources in the reference collection where you can find the answer, but what you need is a quick answer. *Almanac of Famous People* is the source you turn to because it lists only name, occupation, what the person is famous for in one sentence, where and when they were born, and where and when they died, if the person is dead. With knowledge of the resources, you can answer that patron's question in less than 30 seconds! It also has special indexes that are very useful, such as chronological by date which allows you to see what famous people were born or died on your birthday.

Length of entry is one distinguishing feature of biographical sources. Another is whether the subject is alive or dead. While *Almanac of Famous People* lists both the living and the dead, a number of sources list only one or the other. You must be alive to be included in *Who's Who in America*. The first criterion for inclusion in *Dictionary of American Biography* (known as the DAB) is that you must be dead. Geography is also a criterion that can be used as the last two titles show. Profession is another possible criterion. To be listed in *Something About the Author*, you must be a children's book writer or illustrator.

Look at entries from *Who's Who in America* and *Current Biography*. What kinds of information does each contain? What are the differences in presentation of the information? Can you tell where the information comes from?

A new volume of *Current Biography* comes out every year. On the other hand, the DAB publishes supplements to the original series once every five years. Keeping information up to date is not a consideration for the DAB.

Scope is an important consideration for biographies. If you picked up a book entitled *Notable U.S. Librarians*, you could tell from the title that it covered librarians associated with the United States who made some kind of prominent contribution to the profession. While our example has a very descriptive title, it still does not tell you everything you need to know about the scope of the book. You will have to examine the book to determine the extent of its coverage. What else do you need to know about the scope of this book?

DICTIONARIES

Let's start this section with a simple question about dictionaries. True of false: a good dictionary tries to list all the words in the language? The answer: that's a trick question. You do not have enough information to answer the question as stated. You need to know what kind of dictionary we're asking about, and we don't mean either "good" or "bad".

The first thing to know about a dictionary is whether it is unabridged or abridged. An unabridged dictionary tries to list a large majority of the words in a language. However, it cannot list them all and decisions need to be made about what to include and exclude. From the introduction to *Webster's 2nd Unabridged*, it says that it does not include words that are "too technical, too rare, too ephemeral, too local, or self-explanatory (1953)." "Too new" could be added to that list, as the language changes too fast for a dictionary to keep up with. *Webster's 2nd*, which was first published in 1934, contains a huge number of entries at 600,000 according to *Guide to Reference Books* (1996). From that same source, we learn that by the time *Webster's 3rd* was published in 1961, the number of entries was down to 450,000.

If a regular unabridged dictionary doesn't answer your need for information about words, then there's the *Oxford English Dictionary*. The *OED*, as it is called, has extensive etymologies and quotes that show the history of the usage of the word.

We are all familiar with collegiate dictionaries. A collegiate dictionary is an abridged dictionary. It selectively lists words, choosing the ones it thinks you are most likely to encounter or need to know. *Merriam-Webster's 11th Collegiate* has about 225,000 definitions, not entries (Merriam Webster Online 2008).

A collegiate dictionary is a good, general purpose dictionary. It can be used by high school students through adults. There are also dictionaries designed for elementary school and middle school.

Dictionaries can be prescriptive. They tell you the way the word should be spelled, pronounced, and used. Dictionaries can also be descriptive. They tell you how the word is spelled, pronounced, and used. A descriptive dictionary will have more alternative spellings, pronunciations, and meanings than a prescriptive dictionary. Most dictionaries are descriptive these days. There are specialty dictionaries, like *Fowler's Modern English Usage*, that still tells you the correct way to use the language.

As in our other categories of books, there are subdivisions within dictionaries. There are dictionaries of slang that tell you some of the ways to abuse the language and the ears of others. Then there are thesauri that list synonyms and antonyms and rhyming dictionaries to give us lists of words whose final syllables sound the same.

The *OED* is the largest collection of quotes in print. However, it is not a quotation dictionary like *Bartlett's Familiar Quotations* or the other dictionaries of quotations. Quotation dictionaries are usually arranged either by the subject or the author of the quote with extensive indexes of key words to help you find the quote you are looking for.

There are subject dictionaries. These dictionaries focus on the language or jargon of a particular profession or field of study. There are many of these dictionaries in print covering all subject areas. Subject dictionaries can be very handy. They collect the jargon of a discipline with terms that won't be included in a collegiate dictionary. They are often smaller than collegiates because of their focus, and their size makes them easy to use. The definitions are also focused on the subject at hand. If a word has multiple meanings across a number of disciplines, you won't find all the meanings here. Subject dictionaries may not be useful until high school, but they are generally inexpensive. Look up a word in a subject dictionary and a collegiate, and compare the information that you find in each.

Historical dictionaries narrow their subject focus to a particular period and place in history, and then list all of the people, places, events, and ideas relevant to that period and place. Historical dictionaries are odd ducks. Is it a dictionary or an encyclopedia or a handbook? Entries are longer than mere definitions, but shorter than what you would find in an encyclopedia. Historical dictionaries may have little use in your media center, but you need to be aware that they exist.

Dictionaries are clearly a very valuable part of any collection. You need to have a selection of them to round out your collection.

DIRECTORIES

The phone book is the classic example of a directory. If you need a phone number, you grab the phone book and look it up. What if you need the chief financial officer of Apple Computer, or the address of the Deltiologists of America? You use directories like *Standard and Poor's Register* and the *Encyclopedia of Associations* to find your answers.

The Internet can be used to find basic directory information or contact information quickly for businesses, organizations, and people. But the directories we're talking about here contain all kinds of information, much more than what we find in a phone book, much more than address and phone number. *Standard and Poor's* lists all the corporate officers, number of employees, primary business and sales along with address and phone number. *Writer's Market* lists the submission guidelines, types of articles accepted, editor, and contact information for a number of magazines and book publishers. *College Blue Book* lists the requirements for admission among the general information it provides for each college in the country. All of the examples have contact information—names, addresses, e-mails, phone numbers, Web sites—but there is something else they all have in common. Do you know what it is?

The information in directories dates quickly. Any piece of information in an entry can change from one year to the next. Multiple that by the large number of entries usually contained in a directory, and you can see the problem. It is for this reason that directories are published frequently, at least once a year. Directories need to be updated regularly to be useful, but you may not be able to afford to update all of them every year. When you look at the directories on the reference book list, think about how often you would choose to update each of the books and why. Which ones have the most useful or valuable information? Which ones would get the most use? Which ones contain the most time sensitive information?

ENCYCLOPEDIAS

Encyclopedias make up the last section of this long but important chapter. Do you know what "encyclopedia" means? It comes from ancient Greek. The Greeks talked about the circle of the arts and sciences (Fennell and Stanford 1892). If you were well educated, you were knowledgeable in the circle of the arts and sciences; and therefore, you were well rounded (Encyclopedia 2008).

General encyclopedias try to fulfill the goal of being well rounded by covering every major subject area from painting to space exploration, from fission to jazz. Depth of coverage varies based on the primary audience of the encyclopedia. *World Book Encyclopedia* aims for elementary through middle school children. *Encyclopedia Americana* is geared for middle school through high school and even undergraduates. *Encyclopædia Britannica's* audience is high school students, undergraduates, and educated adults.

Specialized or subject encyclopedias narrow their subject focus, and therefore can provide greater depth of coverage, but they still try to provide complete coverage of that subject. Some subjects are broader than others. *The McGraw-Hill Encyclopedia of Science and Technology* has a lot of ground to cover, whereas *Gale Encyclopedia of Childhood and Adolescence* has a much more focused topic. As with general encyclopedias, subject encyclopedias can be one volume or many volumes. *The Dictionary of Art* runs 34 volumes, and the *Encyclopedia of Volcanoes* is one volume.

Articles in encyclopedias are longer than articles in other reference sources. In many cases, all but the shortest articles are signed, and often contain references to other articles in the encyclopedia and a bibliography of other sources. Color illustrations are numerous in encyclopedias aimed at a younger audience. The illustration count gets smaller as the audience gets older and color gives way to black and white.

The New Grove Dictionary of Music and Musician is a 29 volume set covering the world of classical music. The title states that it is a dictionary. Is it a dictionary or an encyclopedia? The length of the articles, authors' signatures, and bibliographies would tell us that it is an encyclopedia. So why do they call it a dictionary? What meaning of that word are they implying with their title? Like all encyclopedias, entries in the body of the work in *New Grove* are arranged alphabetically by topic. This is called a dictionary arrangement, and is the source of "dictionary" in the title.

General encyclopedias are often published annually, but at about $ 1,000 each, very few libraries update their general encyclopedias every year.

The publishing schedule for subject encyclopedias is sporadic: some may publish a new edition on a regular basis; some may publish yearbooks or supplements to keep the original set up to date and delay the need for new editions; some may never be updated in any way.

There is another source that may not be thought of as an encyclopedia, but it fits best here. *Masterplots* is a very popular resource for high school students. While students primarily use *Masterplots* for the plot summaries of novels, it also contains lists of characters and an analysis of each book. The entries are arranged alphabetically by title of the novel and each entry is multiple pages long. Does this sound like an encyclopedia to you, or do you think it belongs in another category?

There have been a lot of interesting developments in encyclopedia publishing in the last few years. Some have stopped publishing print editions in favor of CD-ROMs and DVDs (Academic American, Collier's, Grolier's), and one gave away its information through the use of advertising revenue on the Internet (Britannica) for a short period of time. Now, many offer Web-based subscription services to their encyclopedias for both individuals and institutions. A good CD-ROM/DVD-ROM encyclopedia costs around $40. That's at least 1/20 the cost of a print edition, but there are access issues you need to consider. As publishing continues to change, we will continue to see non-print options for obtaining encyclopedias and other reference resources. Think about some of the books in your reference collection. Would they make a good electronic resource? How much would you be willing to pay for the electronic version?

Then there is the Wikipedia (http://www.wikipedia.org). It is the 800 pound gorilla of encyclopedias. It changed our understanding of what an encyclopedia is. It is loved by some and hated by others. However, chances are your students know about it and use it. So you should, too. The knock against Wikipedia is that anyone can write an entry and that some entries contain factual errors. On the other side, Wikipedia has more entries than any other encyclopedia, more than 2.6 million articles compared to the print edition of *Encyclopædia Britannica* which has 65,000 articles (2007 Encyclopædia Britannica 2008), and because there are many authors who take responsibility for an entry, errors are corrected as soon as they arise, and the entry is kept up to date. Britannica has responded to Wikipedia by adding Wikipedia-like features to its online encyclopedia (Bibel 2008). The link provided above for Wikipedia is to the language selection page. There are many, many languages represented, and many of these encyclopedia have more than 100,000 entries. Foreign language encyclopedia are generally expensive and beyond the budgets of school library media centers, but with the Wikipedias, you can offer your students a reference source in any language they need.

Last, the Wikipedia presents a good teaching opportunity. You can stress to your students that the Wikipedia cannot be the only source they use for their reports, that they need to confirm the information they find in the Wikipedia with another source in your library.

REFERENCE BOOK LIST

Your students' ability to reach the nine information literacy standards from *Information Power* is certainly aided by your setting up a good print reference collection. All three of the basic stages of student information literacy will be greatly facilitated. From learning to access and evaluate information, to becoming more independent in their learning and even in generating and sharing ideas and information with the community, your ability to select effective reference sources is a vital part of achieving information literacy at your school.

The items on this list represent examples of the seven types of reference books we examined. This list is not intended as a collection development guide. While most of the items are excellent, they are not all appropriate to every school library. If you need a dictionary for your elementary school library, you are not going to buy the OED. But you should know that sources like the OED exist.

Almanacs, Yearbooks & Handbooks	**LC #**	**DD #**
Almanac of American Politics	JK 271	328
Guinness World Records	AG 243	031
Occupational Outlook Handbook	HF 5382	331
Oxford Companion to American Theatre	PN 2220	792
Places Rated Almanac	HN 60	307
Statesman's Yearbook	JA 51	320
Statistical Abstract of the United States	HA 202	317
United States Government Manual	JK 421	353
Weather Almanac	QC 983	551
World Almanac and Book of Facts	AY 67	317

Atlases & Gazetteers		
Columbia Gazetteer of the World	G 103.5	910
Merriam-Webster's Geographical Dictionary	G 103.5	910
National Geographic World Atlas for Young Explorers	G 1021	912
Oxford New Concise World Atlas	G 1021	912
Prentice Hall Atlas of World History	G 1030	911
Rand McNally Road Atlas	G 1201	629
Times Comprehensive Atlas of the World	G 1021	912
Utah Atlas & Gazetteer	G 1515	912

Bibliographies	**LC #**	**DD #**
A to Zoo	PN 1009	011
American Reference Books Annual	Z 1035.1	011
Best Books for Children	PN 1009	011
Best Books for Young Adults	PN 1009	028
Children's Catalog	Z 1037	011
Magazines for Libraries	Z 6941	050
Newbery and Caldecott Awards 2008	Z 1037	011
Sequels	Z 5917	016

Biographies		
American Men & Women of Science	Q 141	509
Almanac of Famous People	CT 104	920
Biography and Genealogy Master Index	Z 5305	920
Current Biography	CT 100	920
Dictionary of American Biography (DAB)	E 176	920
Something About the Author	PN 451	028
Who's Who in America	E 176	920

Dictionaries		
Bartlett's Familiar Quotations	PN 6081	081
Dictionary of British History	DA 34	941
Dictionary of Psychology	BF 31	150
Dictionary of Superstitions	BF 1775	001
Facts on File Dictionary of Astronomy	QB 14	520
Merriam-Webster's Collegiate Dictionary	PE 1628	423
Merriam-Webster's Elementary Dictionary	PE 1628.5	423
Merriam-Webster's Intermediate Dictionary	PE 1628.5	423
Merriam-Webster's School Dictionary	PE 1628.5	423
Oxford English Dictionary	PE 1625	423
Random House Webster's Unabridged Dictionary	PE 1625	423
Scholastic Student Thesaurus	PE 1592	423
Webster's Third . . . Dictionary of the English Language, Unabridged	PE 1625	423
Scholastic Rhyming Dictionary	PE 1519	423

Directories		
College Blue Book	L 90	378
Encyclopedia of Associations	AS 22	060
Europa World of Learning	AS 2	060
Mobile Travel Guide	GV 1024	917
Patterson's American Education	L 901	370
Standard & Poor's Register of Corporations, Directors and Executives	HG 4057	332
Telephone Books		
2008 Children's Writer's & Illustrator's Market	PN 147.5	070

Encyclopedias		
Dictionary of Art	N 31	703
Encyclopedia of African American Culture & History	E 185	973
Encyclopædia Britannica	AE 5	031
Encyclopedia Americana	AE 5	031
Encyclopedia of Latin American History and Culture	F 1406	980
Encyclopedia of Popular Music	ML 102	781
Encyclopedia of Extreme Sports	GV 749.7	796
Gale Encyclopedia of Multicultural America	E 184	305
Lands and Peoples	G 133	910
Masterplots	PN 44	809
McGraw-Hill Encyclopedia of Science and Technology	Q 121	503
National Geographic Encyclopedia of Animals	QL 7	590
New Grove Dictionary of Music and Musicians	ML 100	780
World Book Encyclopedia	AE 5	031

Chapter 5

The Reference Experience

In this chapter we will examine reference work and the reference transaction with a focus on the reference interview, and we will look at the ways reference services can be provided.

WHAT DOES A REFERENCE LIBRARIAN DO?

The job of the reference librarian has not changed much over the years. This statement may seem a little odd, but what we do, fundamentally, is the same as what we were doing 10, 20, and 50 years ago. We help our customers get the most they can out of our libraries. We do this in a number of ways. We provide answers to questions from our collection of reliable sources. We help our customers find materials that answer their information need, and we instruct them in the effective and efficient use of library resources.

The job description of the reference librarian as "professional question answerer" is unique. Your job description may not use that phrase, but something to that effect is in there. We get paid to answer questions. That's what reference librarians do. The specifics of how we go about doing that may be laid out in policy, but we provide services to find answers or help our customers find answers to their questions. Interestingly, the people who ask us questions are often involved in paying some part of our salary through tuition or taxes.

One of our responsibilities as school librarians is to help our students become information literate. When a student asks a reference question, we have the perfect opportunity to teach them information literacy skills while answering their information need. It's called the "teachable moment." It's that time when the student's interest and need are high, and so too is their willingness to learn. It's a moment all teach cherish, and one we reference librarians get to experience often and need to take fullest advantage of during the reference transaction.

THE REFERENCE TRANSACTION

Whether you are a school media specialist, a public librarian, an academic librarian, or a corporate information specialist, you need to develop your interview skills to a very high degree if you want to be a good at your job. This is one aspect of librarianship that is sometimes overlooked with the wealth of resources we all have to learn, but it is at the heart of being a good librarian.

The elements of the reference transaction, built upon the model by Jesse H. Shera (1976), are outlined in the flowchart below.

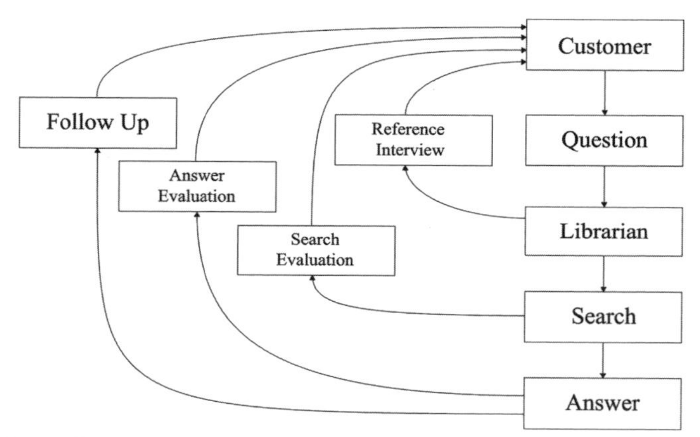

Figure 5.1. The Reference Transaction

The elements are

- Customer
- Question
- Librarian
- Reference Interview
- Search
- Search Evaluation
- Answer
- Answer Evaluation
- Follow-up

Let's take a look at each of these terms, and then focus more on the reference interview.

Customer

The customer is a student or a teacher. Without a customer, we would not have to worry about this whole process. The student or teacher usually poses a question to the media specialist in person, but could ask remotely via the telephone, e-mail, or even virtual reference. The school media specialist is always concerned with helping the customer become information literate according to the Information Literacy Standards for Student Learning (*Information Power* 1998).

There are many people who believe that "customer" is the correct term for the people who use our libraries (Hernon and Altman 1998). The idea is that our other terms for these people, such as user and patron, can be considered derogatory, but more importantly, by calling them customers, we acknowledge our relationship to them. It's not important what we call our customers. It's important to remember that we are in a service profession, and we need to do the best we can for our customers in a professional manner to earn their respect and repeat business. Because school libraries deal almost exclusively with either students or teachers, we will use those terms most often.

Question

The question is the information need that the customer or student wants answered. We will expand on this step later in the chapter, because it is at this point that the process of the reference interview begins.

There is an old library motto: There are no stupid questions. The motto illustrates an attitude that we as reference librarians need to follow. If someone is willing to ask you a question, you should be willing to guide them to an answer. A good school media specialist will, however, often do more than simply provide an answer to the student's question. She will want to help a student learn to find answers and solve problems for themselves. Remember our discussion from Chapter 2? A reference encounter is an opportunity to help students reach those nine information literacy skills.

Information Power (1998) lists 10 additional learning and teaching principles that are meant to help guide a media program in meeting the nine information literacy standards for student learning. All of these lists of standards can be a little confusing, but both sets of standards are extremely relevant as we discuss the school media specialist's responsibilities in relation to a student inquiry.

The nine information literacy standards for student learning represent the skills and attitudes we want our students to acquire. The 10 learning and teaching principles are suggestions about how our media program can teach those standards to students. The 10 learning and teaching principles include focusing on integrating our efforts into the curriculum, collaborating with other teachers, encouraging students to pursue learning on their own, teaching students to pose better questions that will lead to higher order thinking skills, integrating proper use of technology, and helping students link to the larger learning community even outside of the school (*Information Power*

1998). All of these principles represent ideas or ways for the school media program—you—to actually begin teaching students to reach the information literacy standards.

Librarian

The librarian is you. You interact with the customer and the question. You bring to the transaction your knowledge and experience—knowledge of the collections and resources, knowledge of how people learn at all ages, experience in question negotiation and searching.

We must guard against bringing our negative qualities to the transaction—our prejudices, fears, ignorance, impatience, or our willingness to judge and censor. We should take each question we receive seriously and do our best to guide our students regardless of our personal beliefs. In short, we must behave like professionals.

Reference Interview

The reference interview is where we determine the exact nature of the question being asked. This is our first feedback loop, a point at which we ask for or need input from the customer. Sometimes this process is called question negotiation because of the back and forth as we try to determine the information need. We will expand on this very important step in the reference transaction below.

Search

The search is what the librarian conducts or guides the student to conduct in order to answer the student's question. The librarian must help the student or teacher translate the basic question into a valid search strategy. The search should maximize both efficiency and effectiveness. The strategy must take into consideration all of the library's resources, including print, electronic, and the entire learning community, that may answer the question. These days, that's a lot of stuff. It's not just the print reference collection but all the resources that can be accessed from the library or from home. The amount of information available can be overwhelming to us. Imagine how overwhelming it can seem to your students! One thing to remember is that a resource can also be another librarian or teacher at your school.

Given the many resources at a library's disposal, it is difficult if not impossible for one person to know everything about all subjects or about all the sources available. Teachers, of course, will be stronger in some subjects, while you are stronger in others. Collaborating with your colleagues for help is not a sign of weakness, but in fact a great strength for both you and your students. Good collaboration between the media program and the school community can help you acquire better resources, and if promoted correctly it can help students realize there is a larger learning community than their school library and help them connect to it.

Search Evaluation

Search evaluation is our second feedback loop. At this point, you and your customer evaluate the information you are finding to see if you are on the right track or have answered the question. If not, then you need to modify your search. You need to consider if you used the right search terms and tried the right resources. You need to think about what you can do differently this time to find better resources and to be more efficient and effective. If you still aren't finding the right kinds of material, then you may end up back at the reference interview negotiating a modified question.

Answer

The answer we give the student is, we hope, the answer to their question. Because a good media specialist is always trying to help her students become information literate themselves, often the answer is more like guiding the student to find and evaluate the answer on their own.

Sometimes you may not feel capable of helping a student very much at all. The reasons we cannot answer a question vary. We may not have the resources, or the question might not have a straightforward answer. In that situation, the customer may have to look at a number of resources to put together his own answer.

In any case, there have been many surveys over the years that asked patrons if the librarian answered their question. The results of these early studies have generally shown that librarians answer the patrons' questions correctly only 55 percent of the time (Hernon and McClure 1986)! This number became so famous that it was known as the "55 percent rule". This was a rather amazing statistic. Some researches felt this could not be true and studied the validity of the tests. A recent study reported in *Library Journal* mentions these other articles while offering the results of its own very large study. It showed that librarians recommended an accurate source or strategy 90 percent of the time (Richardson 2002). Further, Hubbertz (2005) noted that "unobtrusive evaluation does not measure the overall quality of reference service" and that the "55 percent rule" is a "spurious generalization." These are certainly much better outcomes for the responses we give, and we need to remember that we are not necessarily trying to provide the answer but to produce information literate students.

There are many factors that influence our ability to provide a correct answer: our library skills and knowledge, our knowledge of teaching and learning, our desire to help students, service policies, how busy we are, and the resources available to us. While no one can give the perfect strategy 100 percent of the time—we are human after all—we should strive to provide the best service we can given the limits of policy and resources.

Answer Evaluation

Answer evaluation is our third feedback loop. It is where the customer evaluates the guidance received from the librarians and decides whether the information answers the question. If it does, we have a successful reference transaction. If not, then the customer should ask for more help, which brings us back to the question. What does it mean if the customer is dissatisfied but doesn't ask for more help?

As the librarian, you need to evaluate the answer as well. Do you think the information you provided answered the question, or did you not have the resources to provide a satisfactory answer? Did you help your customer become more information literate? Did you meet the service goals and reference philosophy of your library?

The best school media specialists always have in mind their philosophy and goals of reference service and then constantly review their service efforts in regards to those goals.

Follow-up

Librarians do not have unlimited time to help any one customer. We spend some time with one student or teacher, then move on to helping another. Frequently, we get a student started on their research, and then leave them to fend for themselves. Follow-up becomes an important tool for a reference librarian to employ, and our last feedback loop. Follow-up simply involves checking back with a student you previously helped to see how he is doing, to answer any new questions that might have arisen and suggest new approaches to a search.

Because a school media specialist is often motivating students to be involved in learning strategies for themselves, follow-up is extremely important to help students stay on track without becoming frustrated. A good media specialist will keep an eye on learners and always be ready to provide "just in time" guidance when needed. Don't wait for the student to approach you again, but be proactive and go ask the student if they need any further help.

THE REFERENCE INTERVIEW

The second step in the reference transaction, the inquiry, is the point where the reference interview takes place. The reference interview is where we find out what the student or teacher really wants so we can devise a strategy for helping them. It sounds kind of stupid, because after all, the student did ask a question. Isn't an answer to that question what they want? Many librarians have experienced a customer coming up to the reference desk and asking, "Do you have any books, here?" Do you really think that the answer they are looking for is, "Yes, we have books here."? To find out what they really want, you have to ask them a number of questions.

If everyone knew how to ask a really good question, one that perfectly represented their information need, the reference interview would not be necessary. Everyone would come up to the reference desk and ask for exactly what they wanted. We would, then, be in a position to give them the answer, or help them devise a strategy for finding it themselves. It seems like a skill we should all have, but we don't. Sometimes we aren't even sure what we're looking for when we ask a question. It's at that moment that we start to think about our information need. Having a librarian conduct a good reference interview helps us determine what we're really after. So until we all learn how to ask questions, a librarian who knows how to conduct a good reference interview is necessary.

Let's walk through an example together. A student approaches the reference desk and asks: "I need to find something about Martin Luther and his impact on education. Can you help me?"

A couple of things about this question leap out. First, it is not the typical student question, which often starts with the phrase, "I'm doing a paper on (insert topic) . . . " where you would direct the student to a database and show them how to find magazine and journal articles to answer their need. Instead the student said she needs "something" or anything or background information. This opens up the realm of possibilities. Second, you recognize that the question does not require a database search but can be answered by the reference collection. How did you realize that? You noted that the question requires a specific answer. It's not as broad as "what impact did the Protestant Reformation have on education," nor as open ended. Even if the student insisted she wanted a journal article, you may direct them to the reference collection first as a means at least to start finding the answer.

The next thing you notice about the question is its combination of ideas—Martin Luther, the religious leader, and education. This should get your brain thinking. It's a perfect Boolean AND search, but if you want to take it to a reference book, how would you do it? Would you be better off using an education encyclopedia or religion encyclopedia?

The answer is an education encyclopedia, but why is it a better choice? Think about it. What kinds of information are you going to find about Martin Luther in a religion encyclopedia? Pretty much everything, and that could be too much information. His views and impact on education may be included but require you or the student to dig through the source to find it.

The better choice is going to an education encyclopedia. It's like choosing the most appropriate database to search. To execute our search in an education database, all you have to look for is Martin Luther. To execute the same search in a religion database, you have to search for Martin Luther and education. Books lend themselves to one topic searches, not two. For that reason, the education encyclopedia is the better choice. You could look up education in the religion encyclopedia, but you would still have to read through the article to find any mention of Martin Luther.

Now add to all of this the fact that what a school media specialist often wants is not just to determine all of this in their own head and give the students the answer, but to help the students to be able to reason their way through the process for themselves. But, of course, in order to help students we have to understand the processes ourselves first.

Work through the examples below taken from real questions at the reference desk by selecting your answer from the first row, then reading down that column.

A student asks, "*Do you have anything that indexes the contents of magazines?*"

Yes. What type of articles are you looking for?	Yes, we do.	Yes. Are you looking for articles on a specific topic?	No.
I'm looking for business articles. You direct her to a business database and help her get stated. Now pick your next course of action from the row below.	Technically, your answer is correct, but you were not very helpful. You put the onus on the patron to ask a follow-up question. You should have asked an open ended question to keep the patron talking and to get more information about her real question. Pick another answer from the first row.	*I'm interested in teaching mentally challenged students about the value of money. Do you know where I can look for this?* Great job! With one question, you were able to get at this student's true need. Now, you pick a database and move on to the search step of the transaction model. Stop here.	I think you know that this is a wrong answer. It's wrong because you do have indexes to journal contents. The indexes might not be physically present, but you have access to them electronically. Pick another answer from the first row.
You go back to the reference desk and wait.	You ask her what types of articles she is interested in.		You tell her that if she has any other questions or problems, she should come and get you at the reference desk and that you will check back with her in a few minutes.
You should have at least mentioned that as questions arise, she should come and ask you. That is at least providing minimal follow up. However, you also missed something more important. Pick another response from the row above.	*I'm interested in teaching mentally challenged students about the value of money.* You realize your mistake, and take her to an education database. It took you an extra step to get here, but you made it.		This is much better than the first option. And it illustrates "standard procedure" for reference service: Get the patron started and remind them to ask you for any more help that they may need. But you still missed something. Pick another response from the row above.

A young student approaches you and asks: "*Do you have any books on training goldfish?*"

What? Of course not!	Maybe, let's take a look.	I'm sorry, honey, but I'm sure we don't.
Good job! You made the library a terrifying place for a child. But then, you knew this was a wrong answer. Pick another answer from the first row.	You do a search of the catalog for "fish and train*". You find nothing. You turn to the girl and say: Pick your response from the row below.	Chances are very good that you are correct. But because you didn't do any interview at all, you have given the wrong answer! Pick another answer from the first row.
I'm not finding anything like that. Sorry.	I'm not finding any book exactly like that. Shall we look for a magazine article?	I'm not finding anything like that. Are you writing a report on goldfish training?
Well, at least you made an effort. You weren't surprised not to find a book about goldfish training, were you? You were also polite and professional. That's good. But you didn't dig deep enough. Pick another answer from the row above.	Nice alternative. The girl seems pleased with this idea. You search a couple of databases and you don't find anything for "fish and train*." Pick your next course of action from the row below.	*Yes, I'm doing a science fair project, and I wanted to train my goldfish.* Yea! Now you're getting somewhere! Your library has a collection of science fair books. You point the student in the direction of the collection and say, "Maybe you'll find something in one of these books, or maybe it will give you another idea. I'll be back to check on you in a few minutes or you can come and get me at the reference desk." Good job. Stop here.
"Sorry, there doesn't seem to be anything out there like this." You tried and didn't find anything. It happens. But did you really do a good enough interview? Pick another answer from this row.	"Well, that was a complete waste of time, huh?" You might be thinking this, but you do not get to say this. It was a waste of time because you didn't do a good interview. You wasted your time and the student's time. You can point out to the student that your search did not work and suggest something else, or if you have truly exhausted all alternatives, then say you're sorry that you cannot help them. But you failed the interview. Pick another answer from this row.	"I'm sorry that didn't work. Do you need this information for a report or project?" *Yes, I'm doing a science fair project, and I wanted to train my goldfish.* Yea! Now you're getting somewhere! Your library has a collection of science fair books. You point the student in the direction of the collection and say, "Maybe you'll find something in one of these books, or maybe it will give you another idea. If you need any more help, come and see me at the reference desk." Good job.

The reference interview is where you ask questions to determine exactly what students and teachers are seeking. You need to keep your tone even and polite to encourage them to talk to you. Ask open ended questions to get more information about what the student is looking for. Can you tell me more about your topic? How much information do you need? Ask clarifying questions to focus in on the kinds of information needed. Do you want books or journal articles? Do you need current or historical information? Finally, paraphrase and repeat the question back to the student to make sure you have it right. So you need books about the ecology of the rain forest, preferably with maps and color pictures?

Remember, you are performing the reference interview to make sure you help the customer find exactly what they want, and not what you think they want. The purpose is to help you help them. Don't be afraid to ask questions to get to the heart of the matter. It shows interest in the customer's request. It will also result in a more efficient and effective search and a more satisfied customer.

Once you have a good idea of what your student is really asking, a school media specialist needs to determine how much the student knows about devising a good strategy for finding that information. Remember that your goal is to help the students become more information literate themselves, so you need to ask questions that help them think their way through finding their own answers. If a student is seeking information on how he might clone a pet for example, you might ask questions like "do you think that the information you are seeking would be found in a book, or a current journal article?" A question like this should help determine where the student needs instruction and guidance for this question.

The American Library Association and its divisions publish a number of standards and guidelines that are available at the ALA Web site. One such guideline, published by the Reference and User Services Association (RUSA), is very appropriate here. It is *Guidelines for Behavioral Performance of Reference and Information Service Providers* (2004). It describes five areas of performance: approachability, interest, listening/inquiring, searching, and follow-up. These guidelines further illustrate what we have been discussing in this chapter. It is important to be familiar with these guidelines. They illustrate the interdependence of each step in the reference transaction, and they give you a standard of comparison for your service skills. Finally, they show that there is no reference transaction unless you are approachable!

The reference transaction seems like a simple process: a student asks you a question and you answer it. But there are many variables and factors involved in the process from what you are doing at the desk when not being asked a question, to how well you discover the student's need and their level of skill in finding information, to using all the resources available to you in order to help that student answer their need. To be a good reference librarian takes more than search skills and knowledge of resources. You need to understand the reference transaction and why it can be an intimidating process for students. You need to listen carefully and ask appropriate questions. You need a positive service attitude and the willingness to try to do your best with all aspects of the reference transaction in order to help all of your customers with their information needs regardless of the their skill and the nature of their inquiry.

REFERENCE SERVICES

If what we do hasn't changed over the years, then how we do it certainly has. Technology has impacted our services just as it has impacted every aspect of our lives. Technology has enabled new ways to find information and to communicate what we've found with our customers. Implementing new services based on new technologies is not easy. Here is one librarian's commentary on providing reference with a new technology. "The difficulties are very great. Its problems are considerably different . . ." (Papers and Proceedings 1907). The citation should give this away. Our commentator is talking about the telephone; a technology we take for granted and assume will be part of our reference services. The library literature of that era featured many articles about how to implement a telephone reference service. In the more recent past, the literature featured articles about implementing and providing e-mail reference, then chat reference and instant messaging, and now virtual reality reference. These more recent additions to reference services comprise digital reference.

E-mail

E-mail reference was the first of the digital reference service options to develop. It was an outgrowth of the personal computer revolution of the early 1980s. Kathy Niemeler reported on a study that estimated in 1983 "one percent of the home users and 19 percent of the business users" would have a "communication option" on their computers which probably refers to a modem and an e-mail service provider (1983). This was bleeding edge technology. How many libraries could develop a service that reaches out to only 1 percent of it customers?

E-mail was simple in that all you needed was an e-mail address. People would send you questions and you would respond to those questions often in a specified time period. The question was asynchronous, meaning not asked in real time and not allowing for real time interaction like the reference interview in a face to face or telephone transaction. This could mean that if you needed to ask clarifying questions, the whole transaction could take days as e-mails are sent back and forth! E-mail also leaves a written record of the transaction, something that can be referred back to for analysis and training. Many libraries developed e-mail reference services, and e-mail reference is still around today. With the advent of the Web, forms based e-mail services were easy to develop and allowed the library to ask its customers for specific information to help them provide an answer. The Internet Public Library (http://www.ipl.org/div/askus/) runs an e-mail reference service and their form is a model of information gathering before the question is asked to ensure the best possible answer.

Chat and Instant Messaging

Chat reference came along next, followed by instant messaging. Chat reference services came into being around 2000. On first seeing a live chat service,

Karen Schneider noted that she hadn't "seen anything this important or significant for librarianship" since the Web browser (2000). Chat and IM addressed the asynchronous problem of e-mail reference, providing synchronous, real time communication with the patron through chat software. Chat software can be basic, allowing only typed messages to be exchange. It can also be very sophisticated and allow features like co-browsing where the librarian and the patron could view the same live Web site and watch as one or the other navigated about that site, or pushing pages where the librarian can send a live Web page to the patron to view and explore. The real time nature allows the librarian to conduct a reference interview. There are software programs like Meebo that aggregate instant messaging services from Yahoo and MSN while also providing a simple chat interface that can be embedded in your Web page.

Chat reference spawned cooperative services like AskNow (http://www.asknow.org/) for California libraries and ventures like QuestionPoint (http://www.questionpoint.org/) from Online Computer Library Center (OCLC). For a commitment of time and/or money on your part you can provide reference services to your customers 24 hours a day, seven days a week! Chat services have the ability to create logs of transactions, an electronic "paper trail" similar to e-mail reference, that can be examined. You can look at the logs to see how well you are doing in answering questions, where you may need training, discovering popular questions so a database of answers can be generated.

While this sounds fantastic, there are problems. The use of logs for performance evaluations may make staff very uncomfortable. Creating a database of frequently asked questions takes time and becomes one more resource you have to remember to search when looking for answers. Steve Coffman, one of chat's biggest supporters, turned away from chat saying that most chat services "are not cost effective" due to staff, software costs, technical issues, and low use. To make matters worse, chat questions take "twice as long to answer" (Tenopir 2004).

Virtual Reality Reference

Right now, virtual reality reference is synonymous with Second Life (http://www.secondlife.com). Second Life is a large, virtual reality world in which you create an avatar to represent you as you travel through it seeing the sights, meeting other people in the form of their avatars, and socializing. You can go to an art gallery, attend a lecture, or ask a virtual librarian a reference question in a virtual library. Sound is supported so that you can actually speak with others and not rely on your typing skills, thus speeding up the transaction. Information can be exchanged on note cards that can be saved are referred to again and again.

This all sounds very fascinating, but right now it is also very cutting edge. The hardware requirements are not insubstantial, and the learning curve is steep. As we have seen, however, technology advances and these barriers will grow smaller over time.

Planning for Services

Technology allows us to provide our expertise and collections to our customers in many different ways, more ways than we can possible manage! You need to plan carefully for digital reference services to give them a chance to succeed. Start by considering what type of service you think you can best offer and what your customers would most likely use. What are other schools doing? Is there a consortium you can join or one you can start? Then consider the hardware and software you will need. How much will this cost and will you have technical support, if you need it? Now think about staffing. Who, where, and how often will the service be offered? What kinds of training will be needed? Is your reference desk slow enough that you can do chat at the same time? What if it's not?

With basic questions answered, you can think about implementing your service. You can develop your policies and procedures that will guide your service to meet your reference goals within the context of the service being offered. You need to consult your license agreements to see what information you can offer to whom from which of your sources. And you need to think about marketing this new service to your clientele to establish awareness and develop customers. Finally, don't forget to do follow up. In other words, be sure to evaluate your new service after a set period of time to make sure it is meeting your expectations and your customers' needs.

The International Federation of Library Associations and Institutions (IFLA) have created the *IFLA Digital Reference Guidelines* (2008) that cover everything you need to consider when planning for a digital service. Don't forget to search the literature and find one of the many articles that describe how services were implemented in other libraries. These are a valuable source of information as they can point out problems and complications that you may not anticipate. Finally, don't forget the RUSA guidelines, which discuss appropriate, professional behavior for reference transactions regardless of the medium.

Technology is just another tool we as reference librarians have to serve our customers better. The ultimate goal of reference service hasn't changed. We will always strive to help our customers find the information they need and prepare them to live in our information society.

Chapter 6

Library Instruction

In this chapter we'll look at how library instruction is an extension of reference services and why library instruction should be an important part of what you do.

WHAT IS LIBRARY INSTRUCTION?

First, let's begin with the name. Library instruction has also been called bibliographic instruction, which is old terminology, and information literacy instruction, which is newer terminology. While bibliographies were of primary importance in finding library resources many years ago, they aren't any more, and we do very little in the way of instruction in their use. So we won't use that terminology. We do information literacy instruction, and we have specific standards we need our students to reach in terms of their information literacy education. However, teachers can do it to some extent in their classrooms. It's also a mouthful. Information literacy instruction is part of our library instruction. So while we show our students how to use the library and its resources, we also teach them about information literacy. Therefore, we'll use the term library instruction.

But what is library instruction and how is it related to reference services? What we think of as our traditional reference service involves a one-to-one relationship between the librarian and the questioner, you and your student. The Web has enabled Aska services and blogs and forums where anyone can post a question and get answers from many different people, including librarians. This is a many-to-one relationship. Library instruction falls into a third category, a one-to-many relationship. It's you, the librarian, providing answers to a group of students at the same time.

You're probably thinking that the students haven't asked a question, yet, and the answers you give them now could be forgotten when they need them. We'll talk about making your library instruction more effective latter on in the chapter. For now, our definition of library instruction is teaching a group of students information literacy skills within the framework of the library and its resources. This can mean anything from teaching your students about Boolean operators and searching databases to identifying good resources versus bad ones, from using an encyclopedia to the ethical use of information.

Library instruction can be thought of as preemptive reference. You are answering questions before they are even asked. However, that's not the point. You don't want to discourage students from asking questions at the reference desk because you have already answered them. You want to teach information literacy skills while promoting both library use and reference services. Library instruction should help "raise the level of complexity of the questions that remain" (Grassian and Kaplowitz 2001).

A VERY BRIEF OVERVIEW OF LIBRARY INSTRUCTION

Library instruction, like reference service, is nothing new. There are reports of library instruction in German universities as far back as the seventeenth century (Lorenzen 2003). In the United States, Harvard was doing library instruction in the 1820s (Salony 1995). This is the era of bibliographic instruction and it lasts a very long time. The rise of databases, first on CD-ROM, then over the Web, changes the idea of bibliographies and makes the term obsolete.

Melvil Dewey, among his many accomplishments, was the first to express publicly in 1876 that the "library is a school, and the librarian is in the highest sense a teacher" (Grassian and Kaplowitz 2001). In 1912, William Bishop (Grassian and Kaplowitz 2001), the Librarian of Congress, worried about the exponential growth of materials that he called the "literary deluge" and the need for library instruction. In 1939, Carter Alexander, concerned about equipping our elementary school students to deal with "modern life," saw the need for projects that "require the use of a great many library materials" and not just the prescribed text book (1939). Alexander went on to say that "Training elementary-school children to use library materials effectively is a cooperative job, its success depending on the teamwork of various persons. These individuals are the pupil, his teachers, his principal, his superintendent, his school librarian, other librarians involved, and his parents" (1939).

These expressions certainly match our modern ideas concerning our roles and the purpose of library instruction. Now, let's take a look at the types of library instruction available to us.

TYPES OF LIBRARY INSTRUCTION

To accomplish our goals, libraries have used and still use four basic types of instruction. First is the library tour. It is the most basic form of library instruction and is frequently conducted at the beginning of the term. Students are shown around the library while the librarian points out where things are. It's short, fast, and you can run a lot of students through the library quickly. It also allows you to talk to the students and promote library services. The brief nature of a tour doesn't allow you to do much instruction, but that's all right because the students aren't likely to remember much of what you said. Tours are often conducted in isolation from course work, and therefore can't impart much information beyond "here's the library" and "I'm here to help you find the information you need. Feel free to ask me any questions you might have."

Then there is teaching a class in library use. Most commonly, this is at the college level, and is a credit bearing course complete with assignments, quizzes, and tests. The purpose of the course is to teach the basics of library use and information literacy and to prepare the students for future course work. It has the benefit of extended time and gives the librarian the ability to interact with the students. Many topics can be explored and explained, but it requires a substantial commitment of time and resources on the part of the school and the librarian. A full course in library use can really give you the opportunity to teach your students information literacy skills. However, they may see little value in it unless they need to use those skills for their other courses.

The third type of library of instruction is similar to e-mail reference in that it is asynchronous. The classic example of this is the library workbook. The workbook is often a library produced collection of text, examples, and problems that students have to work through on their own and at their own pace within a specified time period like a semester. When the student is done, the librarian grades the workbook and the student receives their score. Library guides, whether print or on the Web, and handouts fall into this category as well. Computer Aided Instruction (CAI) and Web-based tutorials have changed the look and feel of the workbook and brought interactivity to it. The purpose of asynchronous instruction is to provide some level of library instruction with minimal commitment of time on the part of the librarian. Used as part of an overall program, this type of instruction can be effective. Used alone, asynchronous instruction may be of questionable value. It places the onus of learning squarely on the students and this may be difficult for some students to handle.

The one-shot library instruction session is the final form of library instruction and is a classic that has been around as long as there has been library instruction. The idea is that a class comes to the library once, and only once, to receive specific instructions in the use of materials related to their course work. The librarian has about an hour to go over the resources available and how to use them. The format doesn't allow for much time, but it does give the librarian and the students a chance to interact and work through examples together. It also gives you the opportunity to put a face to the library and promote library services. When done early in the term, well before assignments are given, this type of instruction is not very effective. When done at the teachable moment, this type of instruction can be highly effective.

The one-shot session can be expanded with follow-up sessions and/or asynchronous instruction. This leads us directly into the next section.

THE LIBRARY INSTRUCTION PROGRAM

The one-shot instruction session is an important tool for teaching information literacy skills, but in isolation it does not constitute a program of library instruction. You need a well-planned and well-constructed program in order to teach all of the information literacy skills you need to address. An effective program in library instruction cannot be done in isolation, either. You need the support of administration and the cooperation of teachers to take you from your simple one-shot lecture to a successful program.

Let's look at an example. Let's say that the 5th grade class at your school is working on a big project about the colonial period of American history. You can have them come to the library once and go over, quickly, the resources you have to help them, or you can work with their teacher and have them come to the library three times. The first time, you go over the basics of finding books through the library catalog and using the reference collection. The second time, you show them how to use databases and the Internet. The final time, you talk about good and bad sources of information and the how's and why's of citing information sources. On each occasion, you allow time for hands-on work and help the students find what they need. You also include a worksheet with your presentations to reinforce the ideas you were teaching. The worksheet becomes part of the project, and you take responsibility for grading them.

Which of these two approaches has a better chance of teaching library and information literacy skills? Which one allows for repetition, more questions and answers and more hands-on time? Which one requires more work on your part, but has the potential to reap greater rewards? Clearly, it is the second example that is our program example.

In putting together a library instruction program, consult your core curriculum and be very familiar with the standards. Plan your goals for each grade level and think about how you can meet those goals through instruction. How many times do you need to have the 3rd graders or the 6th graders in the library to achieve your goals?

Think about how you will work with the teachers in your school. How can you get them to include a library component in enough of their assignments to meet your instruction goals? We know what's in this for you, but what are you going to offer them? You can help them create assignments and create the library portion of those assignments. Be sure to tell them that collaboration leads to "more authentic assignments and more significant and meaningful achievement" (Gross and Kientz 1999), also known as better assignments. You can offer to grade and/or evaluate the library portion of these assignments.

Think about how you will sell your instruction program to the administration. Getting the principal on board will make it easier to recruit teachers if they see that the administration values information literacy. Talk about the importance of information literacy skills to all curriculum areas and the value of lifelong learning that they engender. Talk about fostering a love of reading and the worth of creating curious, questioning, seeking, critically thinking students. And if that isn't enough, talk about the positive impact of the library and its instruction program on standardized test scores (Lance 2002).

When planning each individual instruction session, keep these same things in mind, but narrow your focus and goals to reflect what you can realistically do in a short time. Don't try to do too much. Use active and problem-based learning to engage the students. Let them use the books and the databases. Encourage students to ask questions while asking the students questions. Get feedback from the teachers about how the sessions went and what you could do to improve them. This will strengthen your cooperation and improve your teaching. Finally, don't forget to encourage the students to seek you out for more help with questions they may have about anything. You are, after all, a professional question answerer!

Library instruction is a big part of your school media program. A good library instruction program requires the cooperation of the teachers and administration at your school. Therefore a good program needs to be well organized and planned. A good program will not only promote your services but also help your teachers with their instruction, provide the students with useful information literacy skills, and promote academic achievement. This is why library instruction is such an important feature of your reference and library services.

Chapter 7

Library Catalogs

We will take a brief and informal look at the history of the library catalog in this chapter. Then we will look more closely at WebPACs and discuss how to search them effectively.

A VERY BRIEF HISTORY OF THE CATALOG

We're going to start this chapter with a brief and informal history of library catalogs. It will give you an idea of just how far technology has come and the impact it has had on libraries. In other words, it will show you just how good we have it these days.

The *Merriam-Webster Online Dictionary* defines a "catalog" as "a complete enumeration of items arranged systematically with descriptive details" (2009). That certainly covers the purpose of library catalogs regardless of the form they take. So let's look at some of those forms starting with book catalogs.

Book Catalogs

Book catalogs were the original catalogs. There were tablet catalogs dating from 2000 B.C (Casson 2001), but for our purposes, we'll call any catalog that is written or printed, but not on cards, a book catalog. It not hard to imagine a monastic library where the monks can no longer remember all the books they have in their collection or on what shelves specific books are located. They decide to write the information down and create a finding aid. They are already skilled book makers, so they write down their list of books and locations in a book, thus creating a book catalog.

The problem with a book catalog is that it's difficult to update and offers few points of access. Let's use our monks in an example. The monks have worked for a year creating a beautifully illuminated book catalog of their library's 10,000 books. They celebrate their achievement, but the following day, a wealthy patron dies and leaves the monks his collection of 2,000 books.

Now the monks have a problem. Their book catalog lists their collection alphabetically by author, and if the author isn't known, then within the same alphabetical run, it is listed by title. This is their catalog's point of access. To keep our example simple, this is also the way the books are arranged on the shelves of their library. Dealing with the donated books is easy. The monks have room to shift their books and add the new titles where they belong, but changing the book catalog presents a problem. The monks don't have many choices: they can write the new entries in the margins where they should go in tiny handwriting or they can "tip in" new pages at the appropriate spots. Neither of these choices is satisfactory, because they make the original less useful. That leaves the monks with the option of creating a new book catalog. That's not much of a choice.

While a book catalog doesn't have many points of access, multiple copies could be made or printed. This is how library holdings were shared in the old days. The *National Union Catalog* (NUC) was a publication of the Library of Congress. It included all of that library's holdings, plus three letter codes of other libraries, usually university or large public libraries that also owned the material. The NUC was published until the late 1970s and was very important to researchers and the resource sharing efforts of libraries. It was the best tool libraries had for a long time, but it was large and expensive and most likely only owned by large libraries.

Card Catalogs

Our monks have been pondering their situation, when one of the older monks gets an idea. He looks at their book catalog with all the writing in the margins and the notes stuck in every place. He pulls out one of the notes and says to the other monks, "What if we wrote each book down on a card, and filed the cards in drawers. Then if we needed to add new cards for new books, we could merely insert them where they belong without redoing the whole catalog!" Needless to say, the monks were excited, and they set out to produce a card catalog.

Card catalogs where developed in the late 1800s (Chan 1994). The first cards were handwritten and a particular style, which was later called library script, came to be used. The card catalog was a vast improvement over book catalogs. New materials could be added without the need to update the whole thing. Most importantly, the card catalog could give our monks and their library users multiple access points for finding materials. For each book there would typically be a card under the author's name, title of the book and the subject of the book, for a minimum of three cards for each book! If there was more than one author or more than one subject, then there were additional cards.

If author, title, and subject were all filed together in one alphabet, it was called a dictionary catalog. Frequently catalogs were split into sections, either an author/title catalog and a subject catalog, or author and title and subject catalogs. This was called a divided catalog.

Card catalogs were quite large, occupying tremendous amounts of floor space. This was both an advantage and a disadvantage. More than one person could easily use the card catalog at a time, but you could not easily share your catalog with another institution. Book catalogs continued in that role. Both card and book catalogs allowed for serendipity. As you browsed for an item, you easily saw many other items that may pique your interest. Finally, card catalogs required a lot of maintenance to keep up to date with all the material being added and withdrawn from the collection.

Computer Output Microfilm Catalogs—COM Cats

COM catalogs were an intermediate step and short lived. They were in many respects not as nice as the card catalogs they replaced nor as nice as the computer catalogs to follow.

COM cats came into their own in the early 1970s (Zink 1977), and were preceded by improvements in computers and another important library development, the MARC format. MARC stands for "machine readable cataloging." Computers were large and expensive at the time and not nearly as powerful as the computer you likely use at home today. Generating a library catalog was deemed a large, complex, and repetitive task, perfect for a computer. Using MARC format, catalogers would enter records into the computer. The computer could then manipulate the records to create all the author, title, and subject entries for a catalog, then output the catalog to microfilm (Chan 1994).

Microfilm was cheaper than printing the catalog and took up a lot less space. Multiple copies of COM cats could be distributed on microfilm or fiche. This was an important advancement for large library systems. It facilitated the sharing of resources. For example, a large public library will have many branch libraries it needs to work with. By distributing a COM cat, each branch library will have access to the holdings of the entire public library system. Consortiums of academic and state libraries used microfiche to create union catalogs that would broaden access to their collections.

COM cats were not economical for small and medium sized libraries. The card catalog continued to rule the roost in those libraries.

Our monks are faced with a dilemma. They did such a good job with their card catalog that they have been noticed by their superiors and asked to create a catalog for all the monastic libraries in a five state region. (You thought our monks were living in the dark ages!) The task seems daunting. It means a big project, a retrospective conversion of all their books and the books of the other libraries into MARC format. It will require a lot of time. The monks ponder their options for awhile.

Online Public Access Catalogs—OPACs

OPACs were the next stage of evolution for catalogs. If you have all your records stored on a computer in MARC format, why print a catalog on paper or microfilm when you can use a computer to look up the record you want? It seems obvious, but computers were huge and expensive, and your holdings were probably stored on magnetic tape and tape drives were very slow. As computers got smaller, faster, and less expensive, OPACs became feasible.

Some libraries wrote their own programs for OPACs and some private companies entered the market. While some OPACs had more features and flexibility than others, all of them let you search by author, title, and subject, just like the card catalog. The advantage over the card catalog was the speed with which the search was done. This sounds minor, but a five minute search of the OPAC could save you hours of searching in the card catalog. There were other advantages as well. OPACs extended access points. You could search by keyword. This allowed you to search for your term anywhere in the title, subject, or author fields. With the card catalog, you could only search by the first word in each of those fields. This was a big step forward. OPACs supported features like keyword searching, truncation, and Boolean logic, which we'll talk about in the next chapter. You could also have multiple terminals hooked up to your mainframe to allow multiple people to use the catalog at once.

OPACs are still around, but they have grown and evolved.

Web Catalogs—WebPACs

OPACs have evolved into WebPACs, or Web-based public access catalogs. To a library user, there is little difference between OPACs and WebPACs. They look very similar and do the same things. Initially, WebPACs were inferior to OPACs because the technology was new. They offered basic search features, but not the more advanced and powerful features that OPACs had, but that has changed.

So what is the difference between OPACs and WebPACs? Sharing. Yes, it's that important library concept, again. OPACs were marvelous innovations, but you needed to be wired to the computer dishing out the information. A WebPAC makes your catalog available to anyone anywhere in the world with a computer, an Internet connection, and a Web browser. Your students can to search your school library catalog from home with a basic Internet connection.

Hyper linking is an advantage that WebPACs have over OPACs. You can put a link to an electronic resource in your catalog, and a patron finding that link can go directly to that Web site from the catalog entry.

OPEN SOURCE CATALOGS

Open source is the one of the most important and recent developments to come to library catalogs, or more specifically to integrated library systems (ILS), which are discussed below. Open source software is freely available and can be modified by anyone. Anyone, that is, with the skills to do so. Examples of prominent and successful open source software packages are the Linux operating system (http://www.linux.org), the Firefox Web browser (http://www.mozilla.org), and the productivity software suite OpenOffice (http://www.openoffice.org).

Open source offers a number of advantages. First, there is no cost for the software. Second, there is no cost for maintenance of the system. Both of these costs can be big expenses with a traditional ILS. Third, you get a community of users who supply support, fixes, and extensions to the software. The disadvantages are that you need a skilled computer person to setup and maintain the software. Depending on the complexity of the setup, this could be a part-time job for one person at a small library or a full-time job for multiple people at a large or consortia installation.

Koha (http://www.koha.org), Evergreen (http://www.open-ils.org/), and OPALS (http://www.mediaflex.net/showcase.jsp?record_id=52) are three open source library systems. Koha was originally designed with smaller libraries in mind. Evergreen was designed for large installations, and OPALS was designed for K-12 schools and districts (Breeding 2008). All of these systems offer all of the features of their corporate counterparts. If you don't have a person to install and maintain your open source system, there are companies willing to provide those services and hosting services as well for a price.

So, should our monks jump into the twenty-first century and go for an open source catalog? What would you do?

WHAT'S IN A CATALOG?

The catalog is the window into the library. You should be able to see everything the library owns through it. When you search a catalog to find out how it works and what types of searching you can do, be sure to notice what kinds of materials you find. Everything should be listed in the library catalog, all the books and the media. Journals are also listed, but not their contents. We'll get to that in the next chapter.

SEARCHING WEBPACS

WebPACs share many common features, such as keyword searching by various fields and basic and advanced searching options. You can search a library's collection by general keyword, title, author, and subject keywords. Frequently, they have a browse search that makes it easy to find journal titles. Libweb (http://lists.webjunction.org/libweb/) lists library catalogs from all over the world. Pick a few libraries, search their catalogs, and discover the features they offer.

The Default Search

WebPACs are very easy to search. The default search, the search you see when you first start the catalog, is usually a general keyword search on the basic search screen. This is sufficient for most of your students' searches. A general keyword search looks for all of the terms you entered in any order in all the searchable fields in the catalog. This is the broadest search you can do and will retrieve the most records. It is not the most efficient search. It may retrieve too many items to wade through in order to find one or two useful things, and if you know an author or a title, you're better off using their specific searches.

Author Searching

The title, author, and subject keyword searches limit your search to the specific field that you selected. In some catalogs, these searches weren't keyword, but nowadays they usually are. If it's not a real author keyword search, then word order will be important. Check the catalog you are searching to make sure. You will have to enter the author's last name, then the first name, or just the last name. If it is a real author keyword search, you can enter "faulkner william," "william faulkner," "faulkner," or "william."

Title Searching

Keyword title searching works the same way as keyword author searching. You can search for any word in the title except for short, common words like "the," "a," "an," "in," etc. These are called stop words. If a general or title keyword search results in more than one record being found, then you see an intermediate results list. It lists the items you found with abbreviated information, perhaps just author, title, and call number, but enough information to find the item. You can click on the link to one of those items to see the full record. If your search found only one item, then you will see the full record. The full record includes all the publication data and the subject headings.

Subject Searching

Keyword subject searching is very similar to author and title keyword searching. Your search is limited to the subject field. Subjects are the difference. Subject headings are assigned by the cataloger who cataloged the book. The cataloger did not make up the subject headings, instead they used heading from a list of subjects like the *Library of Congress Subject Headings*. Knowing these headings will help you to do a good search, but not many people know them off the top of their heads. Let's say you want to find materials on tobacco industry regulations in the United States. You do a keyword subject search for "tobacco" and are taken to an intermediate results list not of items, but of subject headings. Looking down the list, you see "Tobacco—Law and legislation—United States". Next to that is the number "4," indicating that there are four items with this subject heading. Click on the link to see the four items on another intermediate results list.

You've done a good search. You think you've found everything the library has. However, if you had read further down the list, you would have found "Tobacco industry—Law and legislation—United States" which has 12 items! Subject searches can be hard to do well. One method of doing a subject search is not to do a subject search at all. Instead, do a general keyword search, and scan the items on the results list. If you find one that looks like it covers what you want, then click on the item and get to the full record. Now you have a list of the subject headings used to describe the item. If there is just one subject heading, you can usually click on it and automatically do a search for all the items cataloged with that subject. If there are multiple subject headings, there may be a way for you to combine them into one search statement. Otherwise, use the words from the subject headings in a general keyword search. This way you will get better, more accurate results than with your first attempt.

Limiting Searches

You can limit your search in most WebPACs to specific collections or material types. For example, you can do a title keyword search for "psychology" and limit the results to the reference collection. This gives you all the materials in the reference collection with the word "psychology" in the title. You can find all the DVD's you have on dinosaurs in one easy search. It's a very handy feature, but depends upon there being codes for location, item type, language, etc. for all the items in your catalog.

Journal Searching

If you do a standard keyword title search, you should find journals along with any other materials in the library with your search terms. However, most catalogs provide some way to search specifically for journal titles. Often, there is a journal title browse search that requires you to know the first word of the title. This used to be your only option, but many catalogs now support a journal title keyword search which works just like any keyword search while limiting the search to journal title field only.

WebPACs often provide other special searches like series and ISBN number searches. Other standard features are a intermediate results screen that shows you how many items matched your search along with the first 10 or 20 records, a number indicating which records you are currently looking at, a way to navigate between results lists, full records and search screens, and a method for marking records for further use, printing, e-mailing, and downloading records.

VENDORS

There are many library catalogs to choose from. Follet (http://www.follett.com), Brodart (http://www.brodart.com), and COMPanion (http://www.companioncorp.com) are just a few examples of companies that produce OPACs and WebPACs. We should say that they produce integrated library systems (ILS) because there is more to the software than the catalog that students and teachers see. There are the circulation and cataloging modules to name just two of the other things an ILS can do.

To find ILS vendors, you can do a Web search. There is also a good site called Library Automation Systems and Vendors (http://libinfo.com/vendors-systems.html) (Osborne 2007). It gives you brief information about a product or a vendor and a link to the vendor's home page. Another interesting site is Library Technology Guides (http://www.librarytechnology.org/vend-search.pl) (Breeding 2007). You can search for a specific ILS company or browse the list and then select a vendor. This gives you basic contact information, including

Web site, but more interestingly, you can click a button on this page and get a list of the libraries using this vendor's ILS. This is a great way to sample many different catalogs in a short period of time. If you prefer, you can go to the library search page of the site (http://www.librarytechnology.org/libwebcats/) and find out which ILS is used by your favorite libraries and then click the link to search their catalog.

A library's catalog is the world's window to its collections. It is essential. No library can function well without one. It is a powerful tool that you need to be intimately familiar with in order to provide the best service to all your customers. You should find and search some library catalogs. When you feel comfortable searching them, ask yourself how they work. How does a library catalog execute a search statement? Then move on to the next chapter where we will look at electronic resources in general. We'll also examine their structure and inner workings in detail. This information will give you a deeper understanding of WebPACs.

Chapter 8

Electronic Reference Sources

There are many, many electronic resources available for use. In this chapter we are going to focus on only commercial resources, those resources you buy on behalf of your students. Many times electronic resources are purchased for you at the state, county, or district level and made available for use in the school library. But, even when the databases are provided, little effort has often been made to train media specialists and educators in using these electronic resources.

This chapter can help the media specialist with the very important job of teaching students and teachers how to use electronic databases effectively. We will look at the parts that make up a database and the general mechanics and language of searching.

WHAT IS A DATABASE?

An electronic reference source is a database of information available in an electronic format and a program called a search engine that provides a method for searching the database. The reference source could be an online encyclopedia, or a dictionary, or a collection of current journal articles that are organized and made available to students and teachers in an online database.

Then, what is a database? A database is a collection of related data items, called records. What is a record? A record is a collection of fields, naturally, and fields are containers for specific information. Fields are such things as

- Author
- Title of article
- Name of journal

- Abstract
- Subject headings

Is a reference book a database? Yes it is. A dictionary is a good example. The whole dictionary is the database. A record is the entire entry for a word. The fields are the headword, part of speech, pronunciation, definition, etc. Now can you draw the parallels between an electronic database and another print reference source?

HOW DO WE SEARCH ELECTRONIC RESOURCES?

Many years ago when electronic resources were new and computers were expensive, a debate raged about establishing a standardized search language. The idea was that if every vendor at least gave you the option to use the standard language, you would only have to learn one search language. The benefits were obvious. With only one language to learn, you could learn it well and search any database efficiently and effectively.

It never came to pass. Database vendors had no interest in it. Instead, they had a vested interest in promoting their own search engine with their own search language. Companies put a lot of time and money into developing their search engines—their unique interface to the data. The underlying database of information may not be unique to the vendor but purchased by the vendor from another company that sells its database to many vendors. The features and the look of a search engine is what distinguishes it from other vendors' products and helps to sell its product while developing brand loyalty.

However, there were and are basic commands and concepts that are fundamental to all database searching. These fall into two major categories: search mechanics and search language. Each of these can be further subdivided as listed below.

- Search mechanics
  - Boolean logic and Venn diagrams
  - Proximity and phrase searching
  - Wild cards and truncation
  - Order of execution and nesting
  - Set logic

- Search language
  - Keyword searching
  - Controlled vocabulary searching
  - Natural language searching

SEARCH MECHANICS

Search mechanics are the commands the search software interprets and how it interprets them to execute a search. It is the language of the search engine—as opposed to the language of the search. It has its own vocabulary, syntax, and structure. Let's begin to look at the process of constructing a good search by examining Boolean logic.

Boolean Logic and Venn Diagrams

Boolean logic is the fundamental principle behind most search engines. There are three Boolean operators, also called logical operators. They were developed by George Boole (1815–1864), an English mathematician who pioneered mathematical logic ("Boole, George" 1970–1980).

The operators are

- AND
- OR
- NOT

We use Venn diagrams to illustrate the Boolean sets. John Venn (1834–1923) was also an English mathematician ("Venn, John" 1970–1980). Venn diagrams help us to understand the function of Boolean operators. They consist of overlapping circles with appropriate areas shaded to represent the application of Boolean logic on sets.

AND

AND is the operator of intersection. It narrows your search results. If you are searching a database and want to find all the articles that mention both wolves and Yellowstone, you use AND. The search statement is "wolves and Yellowstone." The Venn diagram looks like:

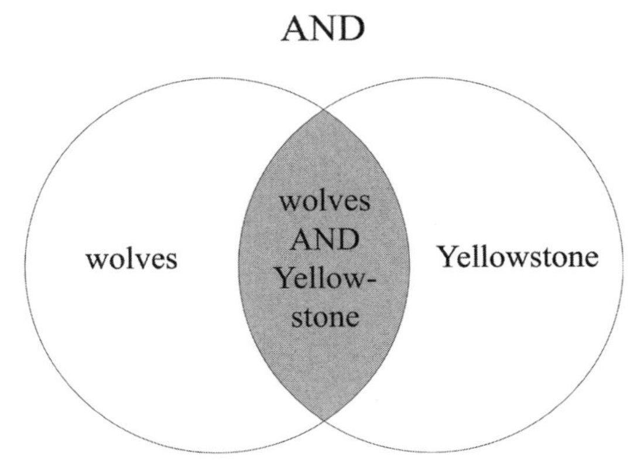

Figure 8.1. AND Operator

Let's look at some imaginary numbers to go with our search. Let's say we search our database for "wolves" and find 500 articles. Then we search the database for "Yellowstone" and find there are also 500. Now we use our Boolean operator and search for "wolves and Yellowstone." Since the AND operator finds only the articles that contain both concepts—the intersection—the results of our search is a set of only 50 articles.

You can, of course, add many concepts together with the AND operator. The more things you "and" together, the greater the relevance of your search and the smaller the number of items you retrieve. For example, you have a student who is interested in the impact of global warming on marine mammal populations. You help to focus his search and you come up with this search statement: "global warming and whales and population."

The database you are searching may have 5,000 records that mention "global warming." It is a popular topic and in the news. There may be 10,000 records that contain the word "population." It is a term that can be used in many contexts. Your database contains only 200 records that mention whales. When you AND your three terms together, your search results in only two items, but they are just what your student is looking for! Below is the Venn diagram for this search.

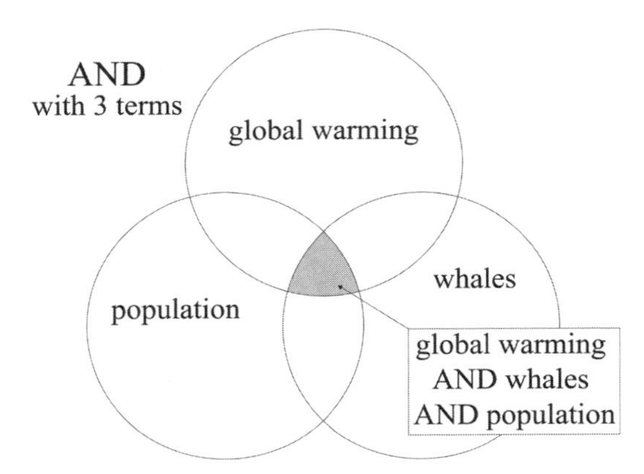

Figure 8.2. AND Operator with Three Terms

OR

OR is the operator of union. It broadens your search. If you want to find every mention of wolves and every mention of Yellowstone in a database, then you use the OR. The search statement is "wolves or Yellowstone," and the Venn diagram looks like:

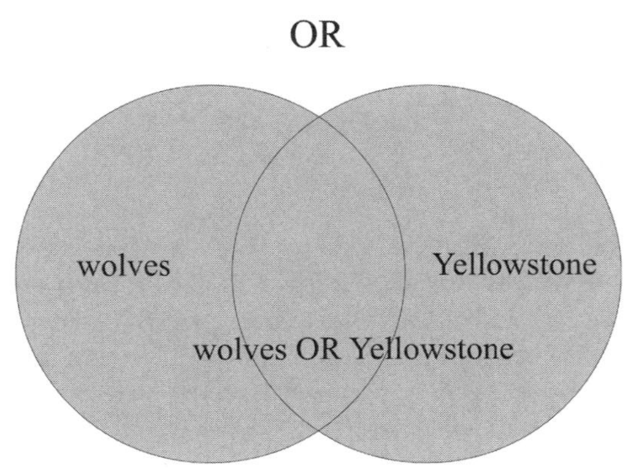

Figure 8.3. OR Operator

We know our database contains 500 articles about wolves and 500 articles about Yellowstone with an overlap of 50 articles. Counting each article only once, this means our search using the OR operator found 950 articles.

NOT

NOT is the operator of exclusion. It narrows your search. If you want to find all the articles in a database that mention wolves, but without mentioning Yellowstone, then use NOT. The search statement is "wolves not Yellowstone." The Venn diagram is:

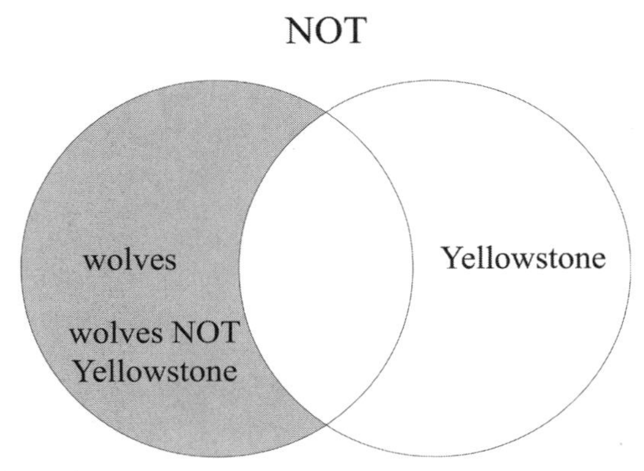

Figure 8.4. NOT Operator

With 500 articles about wolves, 500 articles about Yellowstone and 50 articles that mention both, our search results in 450 articles about wolves with no association to Yellowstone. All the articles that mention Yellowstone are eliminated whether they overlap or not.

AND" and OR are standardized across databases. They are always the same. NOT" sometimes, though not often, shows up as ANDNOT or XOR". You need to check the database to see how it implements the NOT operator.

Proximity and Phrase Searching

Excellent searches can be constructed using only the Boolean operators. But even the best searches generate false hits, records that while containing your search terms are not relevant to your search. In very large databases or especially when searching full text databases, the number of false hits you receive will be higher.

One method to increase the accuracy of a search and reduce the number of false hits is to use proximity operators and phrase searching. Proximity operators work by looking for your search terms in close relationship to each other.

While Boolean operators are standardized, proximity operators are not and vary from database to database. You need to check the help screens of the database you are using to find their proximity operators.

That said; let's examine this example of a proximity search:

- wolves w/5 population

This search will look for the word "wolves" within five words of the word "population." The "w," in this case, stands for "within." You can change the number to reflect how close or far apart the search terms can be. In our example, w/# has an order requirement. What this means is that "wolves" must show up first, then the word "population" must follow.

There are proximity operators where order is not required. We will use n/# to represent this operator. An example would be:

- wolves n/4 population

This search is very similar to the above. "Wolves" must be within four words of "population;" however, it does not matter which word comes first. They can be in any order. The "n" stands for "near."

There are other proximity operators; some may or may not be implemented in the search software that you are using. There are operators that require the search terms to appear adjacent to each other, in the same field, within the same sentence, or within the same paragraph, and all may have complements that require the terms appear in the order specified.

In the example of "wolves w/5 Yellowstone," stop words are usually not counted as words separating the search terms. Stop words are words that are used by the search software to execute commands such as "and," "or," "with," and "in," and also very common words in the language like "the," "it," "a," and "an."

Proximity searching can be a powerful tool. It can also be confusing. Proximity operators are a more limiting version of the "and" operator, and may be of limited value to you and your students. Phrase searching is also a very powerful tool, and it is much easier for you and your students to understand and use.

Phrase searching obviously allows you to search for phrases. It has a very standard implementation across vendors' search software. The phrase operator is the double quotation mark. Anything enclosed within quotes will be searched for as a phrase. A search for "economic conditions" will find only those articles where that exact phrase is found. In other words, only those articles where "economic" appears first and is adjacent to "conditions" will be retrieved. If it sounds like a proximity search, that's because it is.

Phrase searching is easier than proximity searching because you do not have to remember the appropriate operator to use, just enclose the phrase within quotes, but it can also be a very limiting search. Phrase searching is powerful because so many of the topics you might search are expressed as phrases: Declaration of Independence, Bryce Canyon National Park, special interest groups, and Tyrannosaurus Rex.

Phrase and proximity searching are very limiting. They have a greater potential to eliminate relevant items from your search. This brings us to the concept of relevance versus retrieval. The more items a search retrieves, the less relevance the items will have. There will be more false hits. As relevance increases, fewer items will be retrieved. In this case, you may eliminate some relevant items from your search. For example, a simple search for "recycling" may retrieve 400 items. That is too many to look through to find the ones you really want. You need to refine your search and decide to use a phrase to narrow the search results. Your phrase search for "recycling CRT monitors" may retrieve only one item, which may not be enough to be useful, or no items at all! In this case, you need to broaden your search by removing search terms or phrases or expanding your search by adding another term with the OR operator. Searching electronic resources is a balancing act between retrieval and relevance—a balancing act that students and teachers in today's world need to understand well.

Wild Cards and Truncation

In order to do a good search without the benefits of truncation, you would always have to search for the singular and plural forms of search terms: "condition or conditions." Truncation allows your search statement to look like this: "condition*." The asterisk is most commonly used as the truncation symbol. In this case, it tells the search software to look for the word "condition" with any or no additional endings on the word. That means the search is looking for "condition" and "conditions," as well as "conditioned," "conditional," "conditionally," and "conditioning." *Truncation is a Boolean "or."*

Truncation does not get you synonyms. It is strictly limited to what you typed up to the truncation symbol, plus the letters that can be added to the end of your input to form words. So, if your truncation was this: conditional*. You would not get "condition" because your truncation is in the wrong place, nor would you get "state" or "provision."

Truncation is an essential tool in subscription databases. Most searches need truncation in order to find all the relevant materials. Truncation, however, needs to be used with foresight. You do not want to truncate a word and make it too short or it will find too many unrelated things or the search software will even give up because it found more items than it can deal with. For example, if a student wants to find everything about cats, you could truncate and search for "cat*." This would find "cat" and "cats," but it would also find hundreds of other words. In this case, you are much better off searching "cat or cats" than you are truncating.

Truncation is also known as right-hand truncation because you truncate on the right side of the word. Left-hand truncation is a very rare animal. It shows up in only a few databases. Can you think of an example when you would want to be able to use left-hand truncation? The electronic version of the *Oxford English Dictionary* allows left-hand truncation so you can search for word endings.

Wild cards are a specialized version of truncation. If you are doing a search for "woman," you cannot put an * on the end of it to find "women." Instead, you need to use a wild card operator. Wild card operators are not standardized.

You need to check the database you are searching to see what characters they use for wild card operators. Let's say our database uses the "!." Our search would look like: "wom!n." This works just like the Boolean search: "woman or women."

Some search engines use the same operator for both truncation and wild cards. Some search engines have multiple wildcard operators with specific rules governing how each one works. It is a lot to keep track of, but you can always use the help function to find the right character for your search. However, as a school media specialist, you should be familiar with the databases that your students and teachers have access to through your library.

Order of Execution and Nesting

Order of execution refers to how the search engine interprets search statements. Search software follows rules for which operators it executes first, second, third, etc. These rules are immutable, but different search software may have different rules.

Why does order of execution matter? Let's say you want to find infor mation on greyhounds and their diets and exercise. Your search looks like this:

"grey hound*" or greyhound* and diet or nutrition or food and exercise

What your search is likely to find looks more like this:

"grey hound*" or (greyhound* and diet) or (food and exercise) or nutrition

Those terms within parentheses represent the searches that are done first, and then treated as a single unit in the main search phrase. The example represents a database that executes phrase searches first, then AND, and lastly OR. It also moves from left to right. Your search found every article the mentions "grey hounds" as a two word phrase, and every article about greyhounds and diet, and every article that contains mentions of both food and exercise, and every article about nutrition. In other words, the search did not find what you wanted or intended it to find at all. A good understanding of execution and nesting is what the searcher needs to know. Your search *should* look like this:

("grey hound*" or greyhound*) and (diet or nutrition or food) and exercise

Parentheses control the order of execution. This is called nesting. Think of the contents of each pair of parentheses as a nest or set. Whatever is contained within parentheses is executed first. The search software first groups together the greyhound statements and sets the results aside. Next it searches for the food/nutrition/diet set, then it "and's" the first two sets together. Finally it "and's" that result with "exercise."

To illustrate this search with a Venn diagram, don't use one circle for each search term. That would get very confusing. Instead, use one circle for each set. There are three sets in the search, so the diagram would have three overlapping circles. Because the sets are ANDed together, only the spot where all three circle overlap is filled in. The diagram is below, and it should look very familiar.

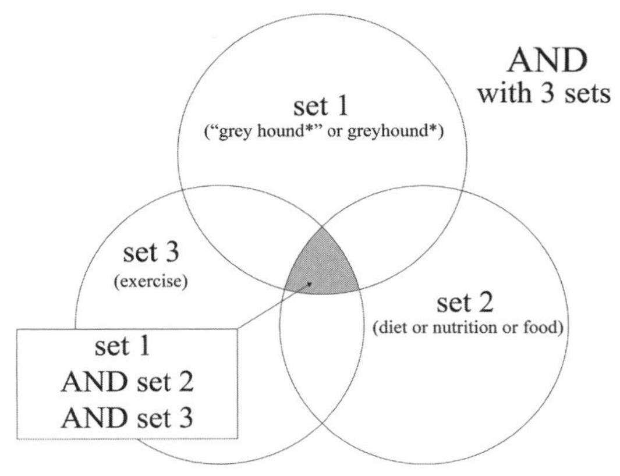

Figure 8.5. Venn Diagram for ("grey hound*" or greyhound*) and (diet or nutrition or food) and exercise

Nesting is a very important concept that you must understand in order to do a good search. However, there is *usually* another way to achieve the same results. *Read on.*

Set Logic

Working with sets is another way to achieve good results without having to worry about order of execution. It is a very good technique to use because it is easy to understand and teach while offering more flexibility than typing a long search statement on one line. However, set logic is usually buried in databases under a heading like "search history," while advanced search screens offer an easy way of inputting multiple sets onto one search screen

So, briefly, a set is one concept or idea and its synonyms, if there are any. Think of the nesting example, but instead of doing the whole search in one step, each nest is searched individually and the resulting sets are combined later.

Let's say we want to search for the effects of pets on the health of the elderly in nursing homes. Using the idea of sets, our first search could be for "elderly or aged or old." The results of this search are stored as a set named "S1." Our second search might be for "dogs or cats or pets," and this is stored as set "S2." Our third search might be for "health or well-being or outlook or attitude," and this is set "S3." Then we combine those sets using the search statement: "S1 and S2 and S3."

Set logic is a good way to perform searches because it allows for quick and easy restructuring of your search. If you help a high school student construct a long and complex search and it retrieves no items, then you have to start over again. However if you use sets to perform the same search, then you can simply recombine the sets. Let's say your search has five sets each representing a concept, but it retrieved no items. You can broaden your search by eliminating one of the sets. Instead of your first search of "1 and 2 and 3 and 4 and 5," your new search may look like "1 and 2 and 4 and 5." You can also add new sets if your search retrieves too many items.

All of the above elements are the mechanics, the fundamentals, of performing searches. This is the "how" of searching electronic resources. Next, we'll look at the "what."

SEARCH LANGUAGE

The language of the search is the word or words you or your students are searching for. It is how you express the subject you or your students want to find information about. Choosing the right words to search for can make a big difference in the results of search.

Keyword

A keyword is the word you want to search. It is also a type of search, as discussed in the previous chapter. The default search in most electronic resources is a keyword search. It will search your word or phrase in any field in the database and then return the articles or items that have that word in one or more of those fields. Finding the article or information you want is largely a matter of choosing the right keyword. It is called "keyword" for a reason. Choosing which words to use in a search is often the hardest thing to do, and you can be of great assistance to your students.

Let's say a student comes up to the desk and asks for help finding articles on the harmful effects that fast food advertising have on the weight problem of children. Here are some words that you could use in your search: harmful, effects, fast food, advertising, weight, and children. Are these all keywords? Are these all important to the search, or are some of these words not very useful?

Looking at synonyms may help us decide. We'll start with "effects" and get back to "harmful" in a minute. Some synonyms for "effect" are impact, result outcome, and influence. Do these words help describe the topic? Synonyms for "fast food" like McDonald's, Burger King, fried food, hamburgers, and junk food are more descriptive of the topic. Words like "effect" are not necessary. They do not add to the search and should be avoided. Any article that is about fast food, advertising, and childhood obesity will be about the relationship between those keywords, or the effects of fast food ads on obesity in children. However, if you use words like "effect" in your search along with fast food, advertising, and childhood obesity, you will not find the articles that use the words impact, results, outcome, and influence. The key is that "effect" is not a keyword. It does not add to the topic. It is descriptive of the relationship between the keywords, but that relationship will be found through the use of the Boolean AND.

So what about "harmful"? It's not very useful, either. It can be replaced by many other words that mean the same thing and which don't add to the core of our topic, but it will limit our results in a negative way just like using "effect" did above. Also, what is the likelihood that we will be overwhelmed with articles about the "positive" impact of ads in this situation? If that were the case, then we may want to use "harmful" and its synonyms. However, in this context, it should not be used. Again, it adds nothing and could make you miss something good. It is an adjective and modifies the noun "effect." Adjectives, adverbs, and verbs generally do not make good search terms.

That leaves the nouns fast food, advertising, weight, and children. We know these are the keywords because if we eliminate one of them, the meaning of our search changes. Think about how these combinations of keywords change the topic and the search results:

- fast food, weight, children
- fast food, advertising, weight
- advertising, children

In addition, when we use synonyms for our keywords, the meaning of the search stays the same. "McDonald's, advertising, teenagers, and obesity" is looking for the same grand concept as "fast food, advertising, weight, and children." These sets of words encompass the same topic, the same idea. This is how we identify the keyword, the best words, to use for our search. This is where your knowledge how to search will greatly help both students and teachers.

Now, let's move on to our final topic in this chapter, controlled vocabulary.

Controlled Vocabulary

Most databases have a controlled vocabulary. It may be called subject headings or descriptors or index terms. The controlled vocabulary of a specific database may even be published in a thesaurus like *Thesaurus of ERIC Descriptors* or *Library of Congress Subject Headings*. In any event, a controlled vocabulary is the list of words created and used by the index's producer to describe the subject of each individual article in their database. When an article arrives at ERIC, for example, to be indexed for inclusion in their database, an indexer—a real, live person—reads the article and assigns descriptors to it. The indexer does not get to make up the words that describe the article, but has to choose them from the official list of descriptors, or the controlled vocabulary. By making all the indexers use this list, ERIC achieves a level of consistency in indexing their articles. It means that every article on a given subject is indexed with the same descriptor, and that means you can find every article that ERIC has ever indexed on that topic by searching for that descriptor. Choosing the right word to search is an extremely important skill, and knowing how to find an official subject heading, or controlled vocabulary term, will help your students to find the information they need on their topic.

How do you find out what these words are if there is no printed list? Databases allow you to limit your search to terms in the subject field. Some databases allow you to browse through their subject headings and select terms. Other databases implement their thesaurus in the database.

The thesaurus is superior to a subject list. A subject heading list is a simple list of the subjects used. It provides no help in finding the right term to use. A thesaurus provides cross references from the incorrect term to the correct one and provides additional information. The *Library of Congress Subject Headings* are actually a thesaurus. With that said, let's take a look at an entry from a thesaurus.

Below is an entry from the ERIC thesaurus ("School Libraries") taken from the ERIC Web site (http://www.eric.ed.gov). The words in bold print are the headwords for the entry we have looked up, school libraries.

Figure 8.6. ERIC Thesaurus Entry for "School Libraries"

School Libraries	
Descriptor Details	
Record Type:	Main
Scope Note:	n/a
Category:	Information/Communications Systems
Broader Terms:	*Libraries*;
Narrower Terms:	n/a
Related Terms:	*Learning Resources Centers*; *Librarian Teacher Cooperation*; *Media Specialists*; *Schools*;
Used For	*Elementary School Libraries (1966–1980)*; *High School Libraries*; *Secondary School Libraries*;
Use Term	n/a
Add Date:	07/01/1966
Postings:	5590

The Scope Note is the usage definition of our term, "school libraries." In this case, there is no definition provided because the term is well known. Next, is the category of the term. This is very broad. This is followed by Broader Terms, in our case "libraries." If you are not finding enough information with the term you are using, then consider the broader term.

Narrower Terms are narrower in their scope. They are terms covering a more specific area that is a subset of our initial term. For our example, there is no narrower term. Related Terms are terms on the same level as our term, neither narrower nor broader, that cover similar or related topics. In our example, "learning resources centers" is related to our term "school libraries." Related terms give you the option of expanding your search or showing you a new direction you may want to take with your search.

Used For lists obsolete terms. "High school libraries" is one of the terms listed here, so it is a term that has been replaced by our term "school libraries." We would know that we were looking up an obsolete term if there was an entry under Use Term. Since there isn't, "school libraries" is still a current term. If we look up "high school libraries" in the thesaurus, we would find "school libraries" in the Use Term category telling us to change our search term to "school libraries"

The final two pieces of information are the Add Date which is the date that the term was first used. It is important to note that date. If it is recent, then there may have been another term used prior to this one, and you'll need to look back up at the Used For entry. Postings tells you how many items in the database use your subject heading.

There are advantages to knowing what the official subject term is. It is a fast and efficient way to find all the articles on your topic. To use keywords to achieve the same effect, you may need to use a number of synonyms to ensure that you find everything, but then your retrieval will be high and your relevance will be low.

One method of refining your search and finding subject headings is to simply try your Boolean search, then examine the results. As you look at the list of items you've retrieved, look at the detailed record for a couple of the items that seem to be on topic. The detailed record gives the basic information that you see on the intermediate results lists, such as author, title, and name of the journal, and in addition to that it gives you an abstract and the subject headings. At this point you can examine the subject headings and modify your search by replacing your keywords with subject headings, or you can just click on the subject heading you are interested in. Depending on the database, this will either do a new search for just that subject heading, or it will modify your previous search by ANDing the subject heading to what you've already done. You will need to get familiar with your databases and determine the best way to add subject headings to your search.

Another method of doing a subject search without knowing the correct subject term is just to take a guess. You'd be amazed at how many times you're right. And if you're wrong, you'll know quickly and you can try again.

Here's a real-world example of the difference between a keyword search and a subject term search. We searched a database for "global warming" as a keyword. That search found almost 17,000 articles. The same words used in a subject search retrieved about 9,200 articles. That means that there are almost 8,000 articles that mention global warming where it is not the focus, one of the main subjects, of the article.

Doing a keyword search is a fine way to search and a great way to find terms that are of very recent coinage. However, using a subject search ensures that all articles on a topic are found and increases the relevance of your search results.

Natural Language

A few search engines allow for natural language searches. You don't want your students to enter a search like this: "I'm doing a report on how smart dinosaurs really were." However, this is exactly the kind of search you can enter into a natural language search engine. The search engine takes the statement and translates it into something that can be searched.

A natural language search is not as effective as a traditional search. It is hard to infer meaning from a sentence, especially one that may not be completely clear. We cover natural language search engines in more detail in the next chapter.

Searching is a vitally important skill for you to master. Knowing how search engines work, and how to search electronic resources efficiently and effectively will not only make you a better librarian now but will also prepare you deal with the changes that the future will bring. Electronic resources are only going to get more popular. The better you understand how searching works, the better you will be able to teach search skills to your students and help them become information literate in this electronic age.

FEDERATED SEARCHING

Federated searching, or meta searching, allows you to search all of your databases with one search at the same time. It's like having a Google search of all your electronic databases. Imagine being able to search all of your article databases, your electronic reference books, your e-books, and your catalog all from one simple search box. This is exactly what federated searching allows you to do.

There are a number of companies that provide federated search software like 360 Search (http://www.serialssolutions.com/ss_360_search.html) and MuseGlobal (http://www.museglobal.com/). There are even open source federated search engines like LibraryFind (http://libraryfind.org) from Oregon State University Libraries. Database vendors, like EbscoHost and ProQuest, will allow you to search all of their databases on your subscription with one search.

Aside from searching all of your resources at once, you can usually configure the search software to search subsets of your databases. For example, you can set up one federated search of your electronic reference materials, another to search your journal databases and a third to search all the library catalogs in the area. Another advantage federated searching offers is the ability to give customers results from databases they might not have considered searching or did not even know you had. It's a fast and simple way to search through large amounts of information.

Disadvantages of federated searching are that it throws off your usage statistics by searching all of your databases when the results that get used may only come from one or two sources and makes it hard to judge if a database is really getting used. If you have databases with limited simultaneous users, federate searching will take up one of those seats or may report false zero hit information if it couldn't get into a database to do the search. Federate searching is simplified to work with many resources and that means that you lose some of the unique search capabilities of the individual databases. Finally, another argument states that federated searching does not teach the good search skill that students will need in the future, and it even encourages the "good enough" attitude that students learn from using resources like Google (Rethlefsen 2008).

Federated searching is a great option that allows all of your electronic resources to be used. However, it has its strengths and weaknesses. Would federated searching work well for you and your library? What aspects of it would make or break its implementation at your library?

SEARCH WORKSHEET

Here's a search worksheet that you can use for yourself or with your students to help you construct search statements. It helps to illustrates the proper use of ANDs and ORs. It will help students identify keywords from their research questions, and it has the added benefit of looking like the advanced search screens of your databases.

Figure 8.7. Search Worksheet

State the question you need answered:					
	Keyword	**OR**	**1st Synonym**	**OR**	**2nd Synonym**
1st Concept					
AND					
2nd Concept					
AND					
3rd Concept					

You can add more columns for more synonyms or add more rows for more concepts, but the more you add, the more confusing the form and the search get.

Here's an example with our earlier search for information on global warming's impact on whale populations.

Figure 8.8. Search Worksheet for "global warming's impact on whale populations"

State the question you need answered: What impact has global warming had on the population of whales?					
	Keyword	**OR**	**1st Synonym**	**OR**	**2nd Synonym**
1st Concept	whale*	or	marine mammal*	or	dolphin*
AND					
2nd Concept	global warming	or	climate change	or	?
AND					
3rd Concept	population*	or	birth rate	or	?

Each row represents one concept or idea. As you work from left to right filling in synonyms, you add an OR between each one. When the search is executed, the first concept line is ORed together in its own set. Now, when you add a keyword to your second concept, you have placed an AND between your first and second concepts to link those ideas together through their intersection in your search. If you had to type this search all on one line, it would look like this: (whale* or marine mammal* or dolphin*) and (global warming or climate change) and (population* or birth rate*). Fortunately, advanced search screens make this easy.

Chapter 9

Searching the Web

This chapter will give an introduction to searching for and finding information on the Internet using the four kinds of Web search engines.

THE WEB

The Web is a huge and nebulous thing. Google indexes 1,000,000,000,000 pages. That 1 trillion unique Web pages! Google ("We knew the web was big . . ." 2008) also states that "several billion" pages are added every day! That's a stunning amount of content! There is no particular rhyme or reason to the Web or Internet. Anyone can create and post a Web page about anything he wants. You can find personal pages, government statistics, and shopping on the Web. When it comes to information, the content, level, and quality vary widely.

If the Web has worthwhile information, how do you go about finding it? You need to use a search engine. A search engine will help you find what you are looking for, but it is no guarantee of quality. Each Web site you and your students find must be evaluated to determine the quality and accuracy of the information it contains.

FINDING A SEARCH ENGINE

The first step in searching the Web is finding a search engine. Try this: type "listing web search engines" without the quotes into the address line of Internet Explorer, then hit the Enter key. Congratulations, you have just done a search of the Web, and you have found listings of other Web search engines to boot! You have used Bing (http://www.bing.com), Microsoft's Web search engine.

You can use this search engine and not bother finding and using any others. However, you are limiting your horizons and your retrieval possibilities. One size does not fit all when it comes to the Web. You can look at a list of search engines with the more popular ones listed first at this Yahoo directory: (http://dir.yahoo.com/Computers_and_Internet/Internet/World_Wide_Web/Searching_the_Web/Search_Engines_and_Directories). You should try a number of search engines to find a few that you like.

One thing you need to remember is that different search engines use different algorithms to find and rank their results. Simply put, your search results will vary from one search engine to another. A good way to see these differences is to use a site like Thumbshots (http://www.thumbshots.org/Products/Thumbshots/Ranking/tabid/116/Default.aspx). Here you can enter a search in two different search engines and see how many of the top 60 results show up on each list and in what order. For example, a search for "supernova" in Google and Bing showed an overlap of 19 of the top 60 items with only three of the top 10 sites from the search engines matching each other.

FOUR TYPES OF SEARCH ENGINES

There are four basic types of search engines:

- Hierarchical
- Page indexers
- Natural Language
- Meta

Each type has its strengths and weaknesses. One may be better for a certain search than another. We'll start by looking at hierarchical searching.

Hierarchical

A hierarchical search engine places information into categories. It attempts to impose order on the Internet. It allows you to browse through the categories. You may select a subcategory within a category to narrow your search. Often, there are many levels of subcategories. The hierarchical arrangement is also called a directory.

The information contained in a hierarchical search engine can be selective. The Web pages listed have been selected by people or machines based on certain criteria. A search engine is provided that searches through the individual listings. The results list is often a mix of individual items and categories. You can follow the links from any of the items to their categories and see similar items and perhaps subcategories. If a hierarchical search engine does not find anything within its listings, it will search the Web at large. You know that it has done so if the results list does not show categories.

A typical search may follow this pattern. First you select "education," then "higher education." Next, it's "United States," then "Utah." Finally, you select "public." At this point, you are presented with a list of public colleges in Utah from which to choose.

Yahoo (http://www.yahoo.com) is perhaps the most famous hierarchical listing on the Internet. The sites listed are selected by human editors. It does not try to be comprehensive, but it tries to list good and/or popular sites. However, Yahoo doesn't list its directory search on its home page anymore. You have to click on "more" to find it. Other search engines have dropped directories all together or link out to Yahoo's directory. This is an good indication that the directory search is not popular anymore and is on its way out.

Page Indexers

All the search engines in this category work in a similar fashion, have similar features, and try to search some large portion of the Web. It is important to remember that no Web search engine searches the entire Web, and none of them search any of the electronic resources that you purchase for your library even though they are Web-based. The resources you purchase are part of the invisible Web. These are sites that are not open and freely accessible to everyone, but have controlled access through either IP address authentication, those computers in your library, or passwords. Page indexers cannot normally see these sites. They search the public or visible Web. Examples of search engines that fall into this category are Excite (http://www.excite.com), AltaVista (http://www.altavista.com), and, of course, Google (http://www.google.com).

A compelling reason to use these search engines is the very large number of Web sites that they index and the ability to construct complex searches. These search engines offer basic and advanced search screens, and allow you to select the type of media you want to find, i.e., Web sites, pictures, music, or movies. To do the best search possible on one of these search engines, you need to know how they implement and use search commands.

These search engines use a technique called relevancy ranking to present the results of your search. If you searched for "core curriculum," most of these search engines used to do something similar to a Boolean "or" search, then use relevancy ranking to display the "best" matches first. What this type of search does is look to see if either search term is present in the Web page, how many times it is present, and where the words show up within the Web page. If your search terms show up in the title or the headings on the Web page, they are given more weight than if they show up in the body. Then each hit in each document is given a numeric value and the values are totaled. The page with the highest total is listed first, the second highest is listed second, and on down the line. This is how relevancy ranking works. Pages with both of your search terms frequently rank higher than those where only one term is found. However, using our example, the word "curriculum" could show up so many times in a page that even though that page does not include the word "core," it still ranks the page higher than many pages with both terms. This would be a false hit. But things have changed; most Web search engines now use "and" as their default operator, which improves the relevance of retrieved items.

The idea behind relevancy ranking is that it helps to eliminate false hits through relevance. Even if you search for two generic terms and get tens of thousands of hits, you should have what you are looking for among the first few documents.

The exact formulas for determining relevance are closely guarded secrets of the search engine producers. However, clever Web page designers know some of the tricks to get their pages ranked higher in search results. This could contribute to false hits or at the very least, pushing the more relevant results further down the list where you may or may not find them.

Google (http://www.google.com) was different from the other page indexing search engines in that its default search was a Boolean "and" with relevancy. Google was the first to do this. Google also looks at how many Web pages link to the specific pages it found, and it uses this information in its ranking formula. If lots of other pages link to a page, it must be a good page. Because of these features, Google's relevance is high.

Scirus (http://www.scirus.com) is an interesting page indexing search engine. It is a subject search engine, which we discuss later in this chapter, but more interestingly, it searches both the visible Web and commercial databases. The Web results are free and you can, of course, follow the links to the sites retrieved. If you happen to click on a link to a commercial site, you get an abstract of the article that was found and the opportunity to buy the full text. This is an interesting development aimed at businesses and researchers who either do not have an affiliation with a library that may own these materials or who do not want to take the time to use a library. Most libraries offer a number of databases from commercial vendors that either are full text or offer some level of full text to their students and faculty. The library bears the burden of paying for these services whether they are used or not. Libraries also provide interlibrary loan services to retrieve materials they do not own from other libraries for their users who want the material, often at no cost. Scirus is an interesting model, but it can confuse library users about what the library owns and has available for use and how the library obtains materials it doesn't own. However, it is a valuable resource. If you needed to use a service like this at your library, how would you implement it?

Many of the page indexing search engines recognize these operators: +, –, and " ". There is no truncation operator because the search engines look for plurals automatically. The "+" operator requires both terms to be present. This is a Boolean AND with relevancy ranking—the default for most of these search engines, now. The "–" operator is the Boolean NOT Quotation marks are the phrase operators and very important to use in Web search engines.

The advanced search features of page indexers allow you to use Boolean operators and construct searches that look and function like searches in commercial electronic resources. You can limit your search to a specific domain, like .gov, or specify the types of files to be found, like .xls for a spreadsheet. There are a host of other special features that can be accessed from the advanced search pages of these Web search engines. The features vary with each search engine. The Web site Infopeople (http://www.infopeople.org/search/chart.html; Barker 2008) has a good chart that lists the operators and features of the popular search engines.

Natural Language

Natural language search engines allow you to enter a search without worrying about operators. You simply state your question. They interpret your statement and then execute a search based on what you typed.

For example, if you ask, "What was the budget of the United States in 1990?" of a natural language search engine, a natural language interpreter parses your statement. That is, it breaks it apart and puts it back together as a search that the computer can understand. Then the search is submitted to the search engine. The example above may end up looking like "budget and United States and 1990" to the search engine.

The limitation of natural language search engines is in how well they can interpret what you say given the complexity of language. If you ask, "How smart were dinosaurs," the search may do an excellent job. If you say, "I'm doing a report on how cunning dinosaurs really were," the results may be much worse as the search engine decides what to do with the words "report" and "cunning."

Ask (http://www.ask.com), formerly known as Ask Jeeves, was a big promoter of natural language searching. It was also a way to differentiate itself from the competition, but Ask is no longer a natural language search engine. Hakia (http://www.hakia.com), Lexxe (http://www.lexxe.com), and Powerset (http://www.powerset.com) are all natural language search engines. They believe that their products will result in better searches than traditional page search engines like Google, but interpreting the language is difficult. A search in Lexxe for "what killed the dinosaurs?" and "what caused the extinction of the dinosaurs?" produced two very different results lists though the questions are asking for the same information. While natural language search engines have gotten better and will no doubt continue to improve, they cannot replace a good reference interview and knowledge of how search engines work.

Meta Search Engines

A Meta search engine, sometimes called a Meta crawler, is a search engine that searches other search engines. If you submit the search "president log cabin" to a Meta search engine, it turns around and submits that search to a number of page indexing search engines, then it displays the results, either combining them into one list or showing you the top results from each site. Dog Pile (http://www.dogpile.com) is an example of a Meta search engine.

A Meta search engine has the advantage of allowing you to search a number of search engines at once. This is a nice feature. You get to see the top results each search engine produced and pick the hits that best fit your needs. It is a good way to find out which of the search engines works best for you most of the time. Meta search engines can save you time but may result in information overload.

Clustering search engines take the Meta search engine one step farther. Results are combined and ranked, and, additionally, they are categorized by subject matter and put into groups or clusters that can be accessed from the results page. The clusters show you a more specific breakdown of your topic and allow you to choose a group of similar Web pages without the need to browse through the pages of results. Clusty (http://clusty.com) is a good example of a clustering search engine. A search of Clusty for "dinosaurs extinction" resulted in a list of about 200 of the top results from the Meta search, many pages of information. However, there were two clusters of Web pages out of the ten shown that went directly to the topic of dinosaur extinction, "what killed the dinosaurs" and "dinosaur extinction theories." Clustering search engines make Web searching, and Meta searching in particular, much easier and more precise while helping to avoid information overload.

SUBJECT SEARCH ENGINES

There are specialty search engines that limit themselves to a particular subject. Scirus was mentioned earlier in this chapter and is an example of a search engine focused on the sciences. USA.gov (http://www.usa.gov) is our government's portal to all the information they produce. It has a directory structure to drill down to find a topic and a good search engine that searches government sites including state and federal pages.

As always, you can find listings of subject search engines by searching for them in your favorite search engine. Search Engine Guide (http://www.searchengineguide.com/searchengines.html) covers a large number of subject areas with many sites listed in each one. Most of the sites are directories or lists of resources.

LIBRARY LISTSERVS, BLOGS, AND DISCUSSION BOARDS

There is another way to get good information from the Internet. You can subscribe to a listserv. A listserv uses e-mail to create discussion groups. Once you have subscribed to a listserv, you start receiving e-mails from the group. Whenever you send a message to the listserv or respond to a question, your e-mail gets sent to all the other members of the list. Listservs focus on topics that can be as broad as school librarianship or as narrow as an indexer's discussion group.

A listserv is not a reference book with facts and answers available instantly. It is a group of like-minded people discussing issues, problems, and possible solutions. For this reason, it is not a good information resource for students, but it can be a great help to you and the teachers at your school. By participating in a listserv, you can read the discussions and gain insights into an issue. You can post questions to the group, get answers to your questions and help others by sharing your experience in answer to their questions. It is a great way to exchange ideas.

There are, of course, lists of listservs on the Web, which you know by now you can find with a search engine. The Library of Congress maintains a list of listservs in its Web guide to library and information science (http://www.loc.gov/rr/program/bib/libsci/guides.html). Listservs are still valuable, but are old fashioned and not in favor. Blogs and message boards are more popular ways of getting to the same information.

Blogs can be created by anyone, about anything, just like Web pages. There are sites like Blogger (https://www.blogger.com/start) that help you create your blog and host it for free. In a blog, the owner can write and post an article, and then readers of the blog can respond and post comments on the article. Blogs are indexed by search engines so their content is available.

It is easier to find a specific topic in a message board than on a blog. Blogs have a linear arrangement going from newest to oldest. Message boards, also known as Internet forums and discussion boards, are arranged by topic or threads within the board. You can quickly spot the thread you're interested in and then be presented with a list of posts on that thread. You can create a new thread or respond to somebody else's post, and you can search the threads to find what you're looking for. Message boards are often maintained by library associations.

KID FRIENDLY SEARCH ENGINES

There are kid friendly search engines on the Web. These search engines prevent inappropriate sites from showing up on results lists. Ask Kids (http://www.askkids.com) uses editors to pick appropriate sites. Ask Kids provides helpful hints for narrowing or expanding your search along with the list of sites found. Yahoo! Kids (http://kids.yahoo.com), just like Yahoo (http://www.yahoo.com), relies on editors to pick appropriate sites and limits its search engine to those sites only. KidsClick! (http://www.kidsclick.org) is a listing of good and appropriate sites for children that are selected and maintained by librarians.

Searching the Web is the first thing many people think of to answer an information need. It may also be your students' first introduction to searching an electronic resource. But there are many dangers to using the Web. While it is easy to do a search, it is not necessarily easy to do a good search. To make matters worse, people pick Web sites not on the quality of the content, but on how pretty the site is and whether they already agree with the content (Anderson 2008). While the Web is an amazing resource with the potential to answer many questions with quality information, it is also a quagmire of bad, misleading, and intentionally harmful information. It is the resource that is the easiest to use and the least understood. For these reasons, it is the resource you need to know well so you can teach your students how to find the good, factual, informative sites, while teaching them how to spot the bad ones.

Chapter 10

Creating Resources That Make Your Library More Accessible

In this chapter we will examine library guides, their role in a school library and how to create and share them. We will also discuss how these guides are changing as our libraries begin to use the communicative power of the Internet.

WHAT ARE LIBRARY RESOURCES? AND WHY SHOULD WE CREATE THEM?

A library resource can be anything the library owns or has access to. However, for the purposes of this chapter, a library resource, or, more specifically, a librarian created resource is something designed to help patrons use the library's collections more efficiently. A library guide, for example, can explain how to use the WebPAC, or how to find magazine articles. It can give an overview of materials on a certain subject or illustrate how to use a Web search engine. A good school librarian notices and even anticipates where students and teachers might need help using the library, and then prepares resources to help them. Although these resources are valuable to have as printed handouts in the school library, some resources are particularly helpful when made available online through a library Web site. Sound and motion tutorials, bibliographies on curriculum centered topics, calendars of upcoming library events, and discussion blogs and other more interactive tools can help students, teachers, and even parents to use and contribute to the success of our libraries.

Although preparing these materials can take time to create, they always save time for the librarian in the long run as they help the library become easier to use and more accessible

BIBLIOGRAPHIES

What is a bibliography?

a. A list of books
b. A list of books on a subject
c. A list of materials
d. A formatted list of books
e. A list of materials on a subject

Bibliographies are an old fashioned thing. They have been around a very long time. In fact, they were a primary way to share information on a topic or on a library's holdings. The Library of Congress published a series of books over the years called the *National Union Catalog* (NUC). It listed everything they owned, plus the holdings of a small number of other libraries. It was a great research tool in its time, and it was a bibliography. With the advent of electronic databases, bibliographies lost much of their importance as a research tool. However, the Web has been bringing them back. Many Web sites list links to other similar sites and some Web sites are nothing but a collection of links arranged by topic. These are our modern bibliographies.

Bibliographies are usually much smaller than the NUC and focused on a narrower topic. As a library guide, a bibliography serves as an introduction to a topic or as a guide to the materials you have on a topic. Let's say that your students have consistently shown an interest in airplanes. Every time a student asks you about airplanes, you go through the same steps in showing them your resources. It's time for a bibliography. You list on a single sheet of paper the top resources you have on airplanes. It is not everything you own, but a good, representative list that will also put the student in the right location to find other materials. Your list covers sources that range from the history and development of the airplane to how planes work and how to fly. It should not be long. It should be one page and can be front and back, but not longer. Anything longer won't get read. The bibliography list is not meant to be inclusive. It is meant to be a starting point.

The bibliography is not a means for you to be lazy. It should be a time saver, and it should be a starting point. You do not just give the students the list and say good-bye. You need to show them how to use it, help them find the first resource, and tell them there are other things on airplanes that you can help them find if they want them.

If you make a bibliography available through your library Web site, it is even more important that the resource is clear on its own. Make sure your library users know that the resource is meant to be a starting point and that you are available for further questions and help.

USER GUIDES

A library user guide can be many things. It can be a map of the library detailing where the various collections are, or it can be a handout on how to use a particular resource—anything you as the librarian create to help students use your library. Good librarians create a lot of these, and they are always short and to the point. As with the bibliographies, it should not be longer than one page front to back, and can be made available both in the library as a handout and online through your library Web site.

It can be harder to keep a user guide short and clear because there may be more information that needs to be included. For example, if you were to write a user guide on how to use an electronic resource like MAS/Ultra from EBSCO-host or SIRS, you would have to be brief and cover the most important features to keep it to a one page, front and back, handout. Again, the guide is not a means for you to be lazy, but it should serve as a good starting point when helping students. A user guide can answer some questions for your students, and help them learn to be more autonomous on their journey toward lifelong-learning. A user guide is also available when you are not. But a user guide is not a substitute for a librarian.

If your user guide is meant to describe an online type of tool such as a searchable database or the online catalog, you may want to use a screen capture utility to create a video of both your narration and the movements your mouse makes on the screen. There are some good free screen capture tools to accomplish this such as CamStudio for Windows (http://camstudio.org) and Jing for Mac or Windows (http://www.jingproject.com). Camtasia (Windows, http://techsmith.com/camtasia.asp) and Snapz Pro X (Mac, http://www.ambrosiasw.com/utilities/snapzprox) are examples of commercial screen capture products. Each of these tools has tutorials and help files on their respective Web sites that will help you learn how to use their products.

How do you pick a topic for a user guide or bibliography? What do your patrons ask about the most? Pay a visit to your local public and academic libraries in person or online. What guides and bibliographies do they have? What subjects and resources are covered? What kinds of information are given in the guides? Do they use online tutorials? What other guides would you like to see in that library? Are there general grade level assignments that are going to be showing up each year? In order to decide on and create good user guides, you need to view your library as if you were one of your students or teachers. What problems are they likely to run into and what is the best way to create a guide that will help them?

Following are a couple examples we've created for our fictional school, Pine Hollow Elementary. The first is a simple user guide to a library. As such, its purpose is to provide an overview of the library's collections, in particular, where things are located in the library, and to mention some important information about the library.

Pine Hollow Elementary User Guide # 1
Guide to the Library

Library Hours

Monday	9:00 am – 12:00 noon,	1:00 pm – 5:00 pm
Tuesday	9:00 am – 12:00 noon,	1:00 pm – 5:00 pm
Wednesday	9:00 am – 12:00 noon,	1:00 pm – 3:00 pm
Thursday	9:00 am – 12:00 noon,	1:00 pm – 5:00 pm
Friday	9:00 am – 12:00 noon,	1:00 pm – 3:00 pm

Need help answering a question, or finding materials, or using the computers?

Ask the librarians at the Reference/Circulation desk!

Circulation: Bring you materials to check out to the Reference/Circulation desk.
Books check out for 2 weeks.
Magazines and CD's check out for 1 week.
Videos and reference books must be used in the library.

Books are arranged using the Dewey Decimal System.
Magazines are arrange alphabetically.

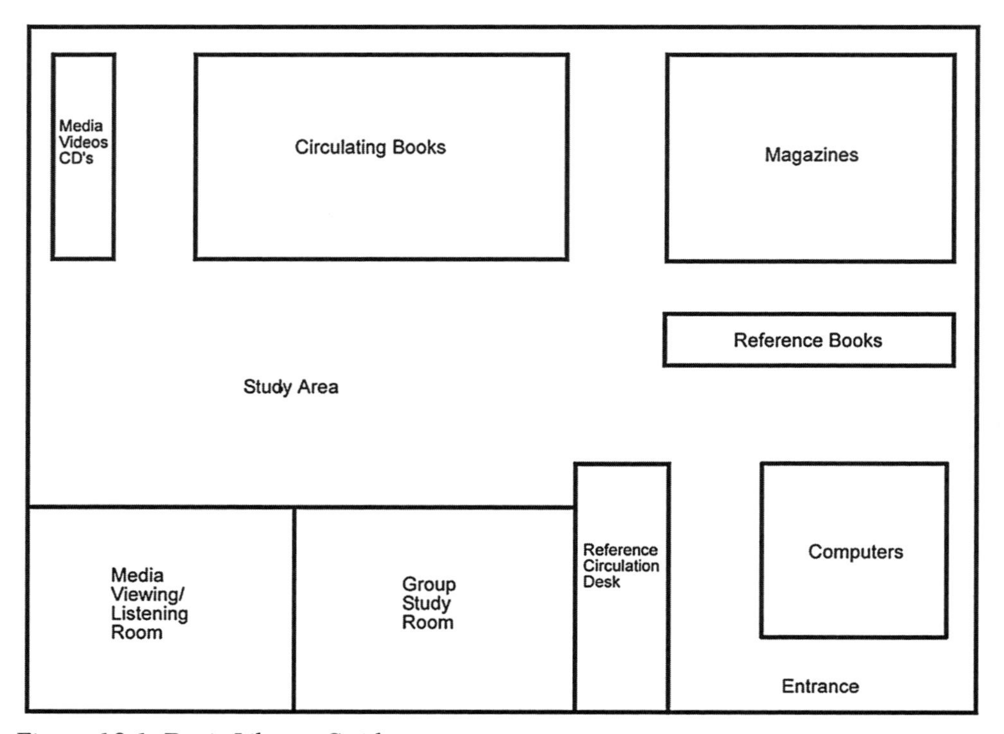

Figure 10.1. Basic Library Guide

Our next user guide shows our elementary students how to find biographical information using SIRS Discoverer. This is a step by step guide that should get our students to an article about a famous person.

Pine Hollow Elementary User Guide # 13
How to Find Biographies Using SIRS Discoverer

The SIRS Biographies has almost 2000 biographies of famous people. You should be able to find information on just about anyone who is famous from "Michael Jordan" to "Mark Twain."

Here's How:

1. Double Click on the "**SIRS Discoverer**" icon on any library computer desktop. Then select "**Biographies**" from the pull-down menu in the upper right corner, or click on the blue "Biographies" icon across the top of the homepage.

2. The Biographies screen appears with an Alphabetical browse.
3. Select the first letter of the LAST NAME of the person whose biography you want to view.

4. Select a name from the list to view a list of article titles.

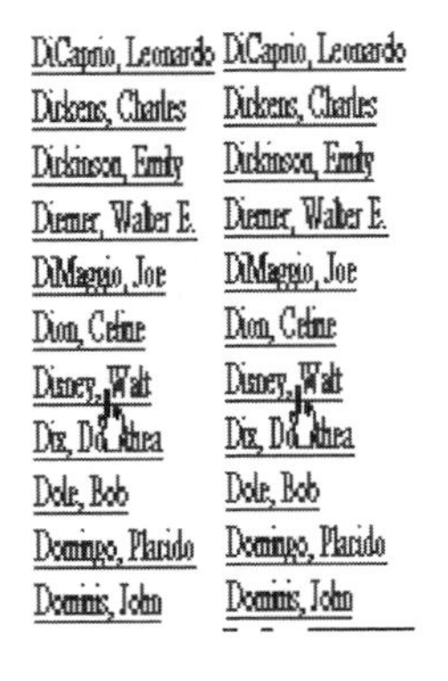

■ Walt Disney (1901-1966) p
■ Walt Disney and His Influence on the Mass Media p

Figure 10.2. SIRS Discoverer Biography Guide

Do you think our user guides are good ones? Are they doing what they're supposed to? What changes would you make?

ONLINE TOOLS

Finally, the Web is a great place to put your bibliographies and user guides, when you have a library Web page. Some advantages are that a Web page is easier to update and maintain than a collection of print resources; it is always available, and it can link students directly to a Web resource. Another advantage is that students and teachers can access the resource without even coming into the library, and more interactive type tools such as blogs and Wikis can be used.

Creating and maintaining a Web presence can seem difficult if you are new to it, but there are some tools that make the task achievable for anyone. First, check to see if your school or district has help available for you. This is the best solution because you will be putting yourself in touch with ongoing free help as you create your Web presence. And you will be using the Web creation tools that your school and/or district are using.

If help is not available to you, you might want to use Google's Web page creation tool called GoogleSites (http://sites.google.com). The service is free with a gmail account, which is also free. It has the services to create Web pages, create links to other Web pages, post documents of all kinds to your Web pages, and many other features. There are many tutorials, templates, and help files available at this Web site that will help you create your own good basic Web site.

Once you have your basic Web site running for your library, you might want to try using some other online tools. Blogs are Web sites that give your users the ability to post their own messages. This is a useful way for librarians to get input from all library users on any topic. A blog would not replace your library Web site, but could be a link from that Web site where students can click to post their responses to a question or topic of your choice. Again, ask around your school or district to see if help is available, or use one of the free blog tools such as Blogger (http://www.blogger.com). There are tutorials available at the site to help with the account set up and blog creation. Once your blog is created, you can link to it from your library Web site. You will have a choice to have an open blog, or require a password that you can give out before users are allowed to post.

Microblogging as exemplified by Twitter (http://twitter.com/) is very popular now. As the name microblogging implies, Twitter is used to post short messages, limited to 140 characters, that answer the question "What are you doing, now?" It is a way to keep in touch with your friends and keep them updated on what's happening. How can you translate that idea into your library? Would your students be interested in following a library Twitter? What would you talk about? How else could you use Twitter? You could use Twitter with group projects where you want to get input from all your students, in your instruction when you want feedback from the students, or for posting questions and soliciting answers. New technologies require outside the box thinking.

A Wiki is another tool that you might want to link to and use for you library Web presence. A Wiki is kind of like a blog in that visitors to a Wiki can post a message, but unlike a blog a Wiki user can edit, or even delete, a previous post of their own or someone else's. This power makes Wikis a good tool to use when you want a group of people to come to a consensus on a topic or learning activity. Wikipedia is the most famous Wiki (http://wikipedia.org) and is an open, ongoing encyclopedia creation project where virtually anyone can post, delete, change entries, create new categories, and otherwise participate in the creation of this online encyclopedia. An automatic history is kept of all entries, deletions, and changes to a document so you can restore any document to a previous stage at any time. This is a useful feature if you find that someone has maliciously changed a document.

Examples of good projects for Wikis include planning activities between teachers and others where they are giving suggestions; making lists or otherwise attempting to come up with a plan together as a group; creating a list of definitions on a topic such as an online dictionary of terms for a class; or anytime when your school might want have a group of people working together on one document and they all need edit and delete access to that common document. There are several Wiki sites that will allow you to create your own Wikis for free including WikiSpaces (http://wikispaces.com) and Peanut Butter Wiki (http://pbwiki.com).

Virtually all libraries have user guides of one sort or another. Stop by any other library—school, public, or academic—and check out their user guides. Don't forget to check out how they have their user guides organized and displayed. The Web is, of course, another place to find library guides. Use your favorite search engine and see what you can find. This can give you ideas for your library

Your library needs a Web presence, and your Web pages are so much more than the guides, resources, and blogs you've created. Your Web page is the face of the library. It is your outreach and your marketing. Another way to reach out to your students and market your services is to create a MySpace (http://www.myspace.com/) or Facebook (http://www.facebook.com/) page. Your students use these sites, so why shouldn't you? You can keep your students informed of news and activities and publicize resources. Many libraries are using these social networking sites successfully. Check out what they are doing and think about what you can do and the kinds of services you can offer. Be aware that maintaining your Facebook or MySpace pages may take a lot of time, but it does allow you to be where a lot of your students are.

New technologies give you new opportunities to reach your students with new services and updates to old services. Which ones should you adopt? Which ones will work for you? Don't be afraid to try them and see what they can do for you. Remember that you are the real expert in your library. You are the one who knows your students and teachers best and can create the best resources for them.

Chapter 11

Core Curriculum and Collaboration

In this chapter, we define core curriculum and discuss ways both you and your teachers can meet your respective learning goals established by the "core" through collaboration.

WHAT IS A CORE CURRICULUM?

The core curriculum represents those standards of learning that K-12 teachers are under contract to teach to their students. The state generally puts together a committee of experts in each subject and grade level area, and the committee's job is to decide what should be taught to children at that level. Usually the key concepts are broken down into standards, and then objectives or indicators of those standards. Teachers are then held accountable to teach those standards to their students. These standards are largely what the end of grade testing questions are taken from, and are meant to represent the most important knowledge skills and attitudes that states want their children to have a handle on at a particular grade level.

Today, the standards and objectives and indicators are usually made available to teachers on a Web site that is maintained by the state. Teachers at each grade level are expected to consistently check the standards and devise meaningful ways to teach them to their students at their respective grade levels and subject areas.

THE CORE CURRICULUM AND INFORMATION LITERACY

What does this all have to do with a book about reference skills for the media specialist? First, just like a regular classroom teacher, the media specialist has an information literacy core curriculum to meet at all grade levels. In addition, the media specialist should ensure that the nine student literacy standards and the newer standards for the twenty-first century learner are being met. If the media specialist teaches regularly scheduled classes to groups of students, then she can meet those standards much like a regular classroom teacher—by teaching students the skills directly. But, if the library follows an open-ended schedule, the media specialist will need to team with the regular classroom teacher to ensure that all standards for library media are being met. The media specialist can do this by scheduling time with the regular teacher to teach the standards to the students, or probably a better way is to *collaborate* with the regular classroom teacher on an assignment that is already going on in the classroom subject area. In this way, a good media specialist can teach the literacy skills in a more realistic setting, pinpointing those core curriculum skills that are going to help students meet their regular classroom goals on assignments or projects.

WORKING WITH YOUR TEACHERS

But this is only part of what a good media specialist is expected to do these days. Not only is the media specialist responsible for ensuring that the library media standards are being met, she needs to help all the teachers at the school meet their individual core curriculum standards too. This means that the media specialist should be familiar with all the core curriculum standards at all the grade levels, and be prepared to help the regular classroom teacher use the resources of the library in valid ways to teach those grade and subject specific curriculum standards to their students.

The responsibility to help the regular classroom teachers meet their core curriculum goals is a tricky one for media specialists, but it is an essential role that media specialists are asked to fill. Good collaboration with teachers involves at least four important elements. These elements are like the legs to a bench—if they are met, then the bench of good collaboration is sturdy and effective. If one or more of the legs is weak or not there, the collaboration bench becomes weak and cannot support the teachers and librarian in their learning endeavors.

The four legs of the bench are

1. A good professional relationship with all teachers
2. A basic knowledge of the teaching/learning goals and activities in each classroom
3. A good collection of the best and most pertinent teaching and learning resources
4. An ability to promote and teach the learning resources in valuable ways

First, you need to develop a good professional relationship with your individual teachers. There are undoubtedly a host of different personalities at your school, and some will be easier to connect with than others. But you can develop a *professional* relationship with all teachers. A professional relationship with your teachers is based on an ability to work together to reach common curriculum goals no matter what your personal feelings toward each other might be. Teachers must understand that you are interested in helping them meet their goals before they will begin to trust you or come to you for help. If teachers don't want to work with you, it won't matter what you know or what resources you have in the library. So the way you act, talk, and otherwise interact with others at your school, your professional behavior, is important to achieving both your goals and the goals of your teachers.

The second leg of our collaboration bench has to do with knowing what learning goals and activities are going on in the classrooms at your school. Teachers often don't even realize how many of the library's resources can help them with their curriculum goals, so they can't and don't ask for help. Knowing what is going on in all the classrooms of your school is probably unrealistic, but we do have a few suggestions to help. First, see if you can get outlines of the weekly/monthly lesson plans from each teacher. Some principals require teachers to submit a basic outline that they may make available to you. Or, if you have a good professional relationship you can simple ask teachers what they will be doing during the upcoming week or month and how you might be able to help. You can also attend the grade level or other team planning meetings with your teachers. This will allow you not only to know what is going on, but it will put you in a position to provide input during planning stages. Time is always tight for a media specialist, but almost any curriculum meeting you can attend is extremely valuable. Your teachers should look at you as a valuable consultant for all teaching at your school, and that can't happen if you are too isolated in the library and don't even know what they are doing in their classrooms.

The third leg involves gathering the best teaching and learning resources for your library. A media specialist is figuratively on a tower, looking out at the teaching and learning trends, technologies, current practices, and quality resources that are being used successfully. Then, within budgetary and other constraints, the media specialist makes decisions about what to purchase and how best to use the new resource effectively. This is something that the regular classroom teacher simply doesn't have time or money to do. The media specialist is of course constantly involved in developing and improving the learning resources for the whole school, which is essentially the topic of this book. Some suggestions to help in this endeavor are reading professional journals to stay current in teaching and learning resources, attending training opportunities, and joining state and national organizations pertaining to school libraries or teaching and learning in general.

Last, a media specialist needs to be able to promote and teach the library resources to teachers and students. Promoting means that you figuratively take the resources of the library to the teachers and teach them how to use them in valuable ways. Just setting up the resources and waiting for interested users is simply not enough. Some states are beginning to call their media specialists "teacher librarians" to put emphasis on how important the role of teaching and promoting is to a media specialist. A good media specialist should seek opportunities to show how useful the library resources are. Opportunities include faculty meetings, staff development days, or even individual or small group appointments with teachers, principals, parents, and students. If you are not actively promoting and teaching the resources of the library, you are not acting as a good media specialist by today's standards. You cannot simply set up a good library and then just react to questions that come to you. A media specialist should act as a leader by going out and actively teaching how to use the library resources that can help the school reach its curriculum goals.

Now take one last look at the four legs of the collaborative bench: maintain professional relationships, know the learning activities in each classroom, gather the best resources, and promote/teach those resources. Are you strong in all four areas? If you are weak in one or two areas, will the collaboration bench still hold you and the teachers well? Examine your goals and practices regarding collaboration to see if you can improve and make the bench more sturdy and functional at your school.

INDEPENDENT LEARNING

In addition to setting up good collaboration, there is one more thing that a good media specialist needs to consider regarding the curriculum. Actively helping your school meet its core curriculum goals is probably not enough. In a basic way, you will probably only hit the first three standards for student literacy and the first three of the standards for twenty-first century learners. The other standards are more about students becoming more independent in their learning and eventually sharing with others in some way. That means you probably need to think about setting up time and resources that encourage students to learn on topics of their own choice that may in fact have nothing to do with the curriculum at all. Some media specialists and other educators feel that our only goal is to help students meet the curriculum standards, but if you really want to help students become independent lifelong learners who will choose to learn for the rest of their lives, your library is the perfect place for them to begin. Forcing students to stay on only curricular topics and assignments with no free exploration may in fact repress some independent learning tendencies.

At the very least, a good media specialist should be constantly thinking about the nine student literacy standards and the four new standards for twenty-first century learners, and devising ways to help your students meet those standards using all the resources of your library.

Chapter 12

Building a Reference Collection

In this chapter, we will give you an overview of the topics involved with building and maintaining a reference collection for a school media center.

COLLECTION DEVELOPMENT

There are many books and articles about building library collections. In this chapter, we would like to spend some time talking about the special needs of the reference collection. The reference collection is an important part of every library. It can answer many questions and serve as a starting point for many projects. It is particularly important that a school media specialist maintains a good reference section, because in K-12 schools we are trying not only to answer our students' questions but also to help them learn how to find answers, and the reference collection is a great teaching tool for this purpose.

There are four areas to keep in mind when thinking about the reference collection.

- Collection concerns
- Electronic resources
- Collection maintenance
- Planning for the future

COLLECTION CONCERNS

Collection concerns include the collection development policy of your library or school district, the needs of the collection, and the costs and quality of the resources available. Your collection development policy may specify the types of materials that can be collected, the subject areas you collect in, and the level and depth of the material to be collected. The reference collection is always subject to your collection development policy, and it will help keep you out of trouble when purchasing items. For example, you read a review of a one volume book on chemistry. The review calls it the best reference book ever published on the topic, and it states that the book is even usable by high school students, but you work at a middle school library. What should you do?

Your collection development policy will help you make a decision. Collection development policies sound a lot like the evaluation guidelines we outlined in Chapter 3. They will mention, among other things, that the material must be of high quality, appropriate to the age level of the students, support the curriculum, and allow for independent exploration and learning. If you would like to compare your collection development policy with those from other libraries, you can go to a sites like "Collection Development" (http://www.sldirectory.com/libsf/resf/coldev2.html). Of course, you can also do a Web search with your favorite search engine and find hundreds of sites. If your collection development policy is not on the Web, consider making it accessible to everyone by posting it there.

Getting back to our chemistry book, should you buy it? It does not support the curriculum in any way, and though it may be the best, it does not fit with your collection development policy because it is not appropriate for the level of your students. You should not purchase that book.

Collection Needs

The questions you receive from students may not always fall along curriculum lines. Often a collection development policy will mention supporting the research needs, or even just the interests, of the students. Supporting students' interests may require you to buy materials that do not fall into the curriculum areas at your school. A good school library reference collection, however, needs to be able to support this kind of use in order to support the "Individual Learning" section of the student information literacy standards (standards four, five, and six) (*Information Power* 1998). How will students be encouraged to become more independent in their learning if their interests go beyond the defined curriculum and nothing is available in your library to keep them engaged? Your electronic resources will go a long way toward filling this role. This means you need to provide instruction that will enable your students to explore and browse these resources on their own. You should also purchase print materials for this purpose to help those students who would be better served by a book.

When evaluating materials for purchase, some of the questions to ask are does this fill a hole in the collection? Does it supplement existing material? Does it supersede existing material and does that material need to be weeded? In order to answer these questions you need to know your students, your curriculum, and your collection well. If you have no books on animals in your library, you need to buy some. If a new book comes out about big cats in the wild and you have a number of books about animals and wild cats, you need to evaluate how that book might fit into your collection. Does it contain information not available in your other sources? Does it have more color pictures and is that important? Will that make the book more useful to some students? If the book does not fit in your collection because it offers nothing new or does not fill any gaps, then you shouldn't buy it. As a school media specialist, you are always looking for the materials and resources that will help your students to become more literate according to the information literacy standards.

Costs

Cost is something school media specialists always need to consider. None of us will ever have enough money to buy everything we want for the collection. Money is frequently tight and reference materials are expensive. Reference books range in price from $20 to $10,000. We need to know if the resource is affordable considering our budget. If there is an encyclopedia you need and it costs $1,000, how big a piece of your budget will that purchase take? What other resources will you be unable to buy because of that purchase? That leads to the question of whether the resource is worth the price. A $50 or a $500 book that never gets used is a waste of money. A $1,000 book that gets used regularly is worth the cost. Cost per use is a common measure of value in libraries. To get hard numbers, you need to check and see if your ILS supports in-house usage counts, then set up an procedure to get those counts. That $1,000 resource that gets used 500 times costs only $2 for each use. A $50 book that gets used twice would have a cost per use ratio of $25. Which one of these two resources is the better value? Clearly this means you should consider more than purchase price when examining a resource for purchase. Its potential use should also be factored into your thinking.

When considering an item for purchase, it is a good idea to check if there is something similar available from another publisher. If there is, then how much does each item cost? Does the alternative make the one you were considering more or less of a bargain?

Another thing to consider when purchasing any book is how often new editions come out, if at all, and how significant the changes are? What's the difference between the first and second edition, or the third and the fourth edition, of this resource? Can you get along with the old edition or are there good reasons for purchasing the new edition? Encyclopedias are published on a yearly basis, now. If you know you want a print encyclopedia, do you need to buy the new version of it every year or can you buy it every fourth or fifth year?

Quality

Once you have made a determination about what reference resource your library needs, and how much you can spend on it, you obviously want to be sure that the resource is of good quality. That leads back to our discussion in Chapter 3. Which questions about a reference source can you answer without having the item in hand to look at? Fortunately, there are many places to get help. You can and should check the reviews. There are journals like *Horn Book*, *School*

Library Journal, and *Booklist* among others that include reference materials in their reviews.

There are print publications like *American Reference Books Annual* (*ARBA*; 2008) that reviews only reference materials at all levels and includes both good and bad sources. Then there are resources like *Children's Catalog* (Price 2006), and *Middle and Junior High School Library Catalog* (Price 2005) that are more specific about level, but do not list reference books separately. You have to read through the entries to find the books you would consider to be reference. All of these resources are also available as subscription databases.

There are also books like these: *Recommended Reference Books for Small and Medium-sized Libraries and Media Centers* (*RRB*; Hysell 2009) and *Reference Sources for Small and Medium-sized Libraries* (*RSSML*; O'Gorman 2007). Each of these resources list recommended reference materials by subject. *RRB*, which is based on *ARBA*, list only materials published in the past year. *RSSML* list both in print and out of print resources.

The Web is also a good place to find lists of resources and reviews. The Metropolitan Library System in Illinois publishes core reference lists for K-8 (http://www.mls.lib.il.us/consulting/MLSElementaryCoreList_2008_11.pdf) and high school libraries (http://mlshsresources.wetpaint.com/), the latter using a Wiki to present the information. Amazon (http://www.amazon.com) allows anyone to review materials. You can often find a review here for a new publication long before one shows up in print. As with all Web resources, reviews from Web sites should be subjected to additional scrutiny. If you cannot find a review from a reliable source for an item you feel your collection needs, then you must evaluate the publisher and author of the item, and the item's potential value to your collection.

All of these resources will help you make an informed decision about items you are considering for purchase. They will all help you build a high quality, useful reference collection. Get to know your reviewing sources and how they describe highly recommended and valuable source. They all have a unique language.

Finally, don't forget another highly valuable resource, your colleagues. Ask a colleague in another school if they bought a particular resource and what they think of it. If they haven't bought it, ask them if they would and why. You get the benefits of their experience, and they are flattered that you asked them for advice. Plus, you'll be building your professional network, which will help you become a better librarian.

ELECTRONIC RESOURCES

Electronic resources are subject to all the same questions as print resources, and they have a few additional questions and concerns that need to be addressed. The first of those unique questions is how easy is this resource to use for your teachers and students? Is it easy to navigate around the resource? Is searching easy? What features are offered with the search engine and how are they implemented? How good is the interface? Does it have a help function? Is the help function easy to get at and use? Does it provide good, clear answers that are appropriate for the learning levels of your students? Does it offer a tutorial?

Finally, the last question to ask is can my students find what they are looking for? You will probably need to try before you buy when it comes to electronic resources. Fortunately, it is standard practice on the part of database vendors to give free trial access. This will give you time to explore the product and answer all your questions and concerns about it. You can also invite your teachers to look at the product during the trial and get their feedback about its usefulness.

Electronic resources are sold in unique ways that requires you to ask a number of other questions. Most databases like MAS Ultra from EBSCOhost and InfoTrac Junior Edition from Gale are leased, not purchased. You don't own the information; you just rent access to it. And just like rent, you have to keep paying it as long as you want the product. Pricing is usually based on type of library, number of potential users (your enrollment), and number of simultaneous users. An academic library may pay more than a school library. A school with 4,000 students may pay more than a school with 400. Giving access to 10 simultaneous users costs more than having only two accesses. Limiting the number of simultaneous users has the advantage of saving you money and under normal circumstances you may never exceed your limit. However, if you show a whole class how to use a database, then set them all lose to work on their project, you could run into problems. When purchasing databases, you need to consider all of your options carefully.

Electronic resources are expensive. Because of their price, they are often purchased by consortia. A consortium of libraries can use its size to purchase access to electronic resources at a reduced rate and save all the member libraries some money while providing them with access to resources that they otherwise could not afford. This is often done at the state level for all school libraries in the state. A statewide consortium will centralize purchasing decisions and maintenance for a number of your electronic resources, perhaps even including your primary electronic resources. A consortium is a great way to purchase resources, but there may still be electronic resources you need to purchase on your own for your library.

Besides databases, you can purchase electronic versions of reference books. Oxford Reference Online (http://www.oxfordreference.com/pub/views/home.html) is a collection of reference books published by Oxford University Press. It is a licensed product and follows the pricing models of other databases. At the other end of the spectrum, you can purchase individual reference titles from a number of vendors including Oxford with its Oxford Digital Reference Shelf (http://www.oxford-digitalreference.com/) and Gale with its Gale Virtual Reference Library (http://www.gale.cengage.com/servlet/GvrlMS). Just like their print counterparts, you own the titles you buy. This means it's yours for as long as you think the information is valuable. Unlike the print copy, you often get unlimited simultaneous users and 24/7 access to the information, but you pay a premium over the print cost which could be up to 20 percent. You may also get hosting fees, an annual fee based on the number of items you own for providing access to the information. It's like buying a book then paying to store it in someone else's library. Some of these fees are reasonable and some are not. You can often choose to host these e-books on your own server, but doing so requires technical expertise.

When you purchase e-reference books, you have to think about how your students are going to find these resources. MARC records come with your purchase, so you can include the items in your catalog with a link to the resource. But will your students know to go to the catalog to find these things, and how would they search for them? You can put links to these individual items on your Web pages. But as the number of these items grows and your list gets cumbersome, how are you going to deal with it?

Electronic reference books are great resources because they are often easier to use than their print counterparts, they require no shelf space, and they are always available. However, you will have to figure the additional cost and the hosting fees into your equations along with how you are going to facilitate access to these exciting resources.

COLLECTION MAINTENANCE

Maintaining the reference collection involves updating, weeding, and stacks maintenance, as it does with any collection in the library. The reference collection may need this kind of attention more often to maintain its value as a primary resource. Updating refers to keeping the collection current, not just buying new editions of materials, but buying new resources with new information. Some areas, like the sciences, need to be kept more current than others because of the rapid development of new information.

You should always collaborate with the subject area teachers at your school. They are experts in their disciplines and grade levels. Some basic questions for you and your teachers to consider when trying to keep the collection current are what can I afford to buy this year? What do I need to buy this year? What can wait until next year? What is necessary to buy for the curriculum? What would be a good additional resource outside the curriculum if money permits? What format will work best for my students?

Weeding is sometimes called de-selection because you use the same reasoned approach to de-selecting as you would to selecting materials. If you have materials with information that is no longer accurate, it needs to be weeded. Students deserve to find the correct answer to their questions in the reference collection, not an incorrect answer. What needs to be weeded is different from what should be weeded. You may have resources that are starting to show their age, but there is either nothing better or newer on the market or you cannot afford to replace them. As long as the information still has value and is not misleading or misinforming your patrons, it can be kept. For example, the *Encyclopedia of Philosophy* was published more than 30 years ago. It was a very important work and many libraries bought it. It is old. Things have changed. There are new philosophers and philosophies, and reconsiderations of old philosophers and philosophies. There was a new encyclopedia of philosophy published recently called the *Routledge Encyclopedia of Philosophy*. It received excellent reviews, and it cost $2,000! While the old set is showing its age, many of us cannot afford the new set. Instead of getting rid of the old set, which still has value for its historical information, you can buy a handbook or a dictionary, or maybe a one volume encyclopedia to update the old set. This might be enough, and it is a lot less expensive than buying the new encyclopedia.

All libraries have limited space and limited shelf space. We need to be concerned about the amount of space our collections occupy and will occupy in the future. This is stacks maintenance. For some libraries, space is so tight that if they buy three linear feet of materials, they must weed three linear feet of materials to make room for the new. Hopefully you are not in that situation, but you must think about your growth rate. The proliferation of electronic resources is easing the problem of space somewhat but creates other problems. Let's say space is tight in your library. So you purchase access to *World Book* online and get rid of your print copy to have the space for other materials. What do you do when you have classes of 25 come in to use *World Book* and you have only 10 computers? What do you do if the price of the online version rises beyond what you can afford? With space, you need to think about how much you have, how rapidly you are filling it and what you can do if space becomes a problem. Planning ahead will save you problems in the long run.

PLANNING FOR THE FUTURE

Libraries have changed a lot throughout their history, and as the pace of change in technology has accelerated, so too has the paced of change in libraries increased. We know our libraries will continue to change, and we can anticipate some of those changes, but not all of them. We need to think about the future, so we can plan for it—so we can be prepared for it. We need to ask what the reference collection will look like in five years and what we can do now that will help us transition into that new future.

We know that electronic resources are an important part of our collections and that students like using them. Will they become more important or have they peaked? Electronic books are being marketed to individuals and collections of e-books are being sold to libraries. Will you be able to purchase an e-book and "check out" a time-sensitive version to a student's personal reader? This may be a significant development that greatly affects libraries in the next 10 years, or it may never advance beyond a small niche. Smart phones like the iPhone and the BlackBerry are basically small, network-enabled computers. How will these devices impact the services you offer? School media specialists today need to stay up with current technologies and resources that may help their students and teachers access and use the library's collections.

Mediums come and go. Our students don't know what an LP is. They've been replaced by MP3's. DVD's have replaced videotapes which replaced 16 mm films. Is it time to replace the videos you currently own? Will on-demand viewing from the Internet replace DVD's?

Because libraries are moving in the direction of more and more electronic resources and services, what do you do to prepare for them? Watch your budget and the pricing of electronic resources, carefully plan new services to support new devices and resources. Add additional computers with high speed Internet connections. Make sure that wireless access is available in your library. The more connected your library is, the better. Web resources are not going to go away anytime soon. Something new that no one has thought of may come along and demand attention from libraries, but the vast majority of libraries cannot afford to be on the cutting edge. You do not need to adopt new technology the minute it is available. It is best to wait and let the technology prove itself. This also gives you time to think about implementing the new technology.

Remember, even if a technology is well established before you adopt it, it is still new to you and your library. You need to plan for its implementation, which means space, money, equipment, training, and more importantly time. Your time is not only your library's most valuable resource, it is its most limited.

How do you learn about new and coming trends? Keep your eyes and ears open. Watch the news and browse the professional literature. You probably have an expert in technology and media at your county or school district offices who can help you with this. If you can, attend a convention or conference, and while you're there, visit the vendors and see the latest and greatest products they are offering.

There are many exciting new products and technologies competing along with traditional resources for your library's limited budget. Building and maintaining a vital reference collection will keep the heart of your library pumping. Anticipating and planning for the future will make implementing new resources that much easier and will keep the reference collection strong and relevant. Meeting the challenges the future will bring requires you to balance the needs of your students with the resources and the budget available to you. It is not an easy task, but it is a vital one and the vitality of your library depends upon it.

Chapter 13

Evaluation of Reference Service

In this chapter, we will look at the reasons you should evaluate your performance at the reference desk, some methods to do so, and some guidelines that will help you in the evaluation process. Finally, we will briefly look at putting it all together with a report that will let everyone know what you're doing.

BEFORE YOU BEGIN

- Determine goals for your reference service
- Set guidelines for performance at the reference desk
- Understand why we evaluate

The Goal of Reference Service

It is necessary to have a written statement of purpose for reference service at your library. This is your reference service philosophy. Without a statement of purpose, you cannot judge whether you are meeting your library's goals for service or not. The statement of purpose guides what you should be trying to do when you provide reference service.

Let's say this is your statement of your reference service philosophy: *The goal of our reference service is to provide the highest quality instruction and assistance to our library users in the use of library resources in order to teach them information literacy skills that will be essential throughout their lives while providing them with the information that they need or want.* This statement emphasizes the importance of the teaching role of reference and de-emphasizes the provision of answers.

Your statement may be a bit different from this. However, the idea is the same. The statement is essentially an outline of the kind of service you want to provide. It is the goal of your service. If you know what sort of service you are trying to provide, then you can evaluate how well you provide those services. Think of a well-defined philosophy of reference service as a yardstick by which to measure your service.

Your reference service philosophy is a guiding statement. It is the ideal. It is not, however, your policy. Any restrictions, limitations, or specific instructions and guidelines that effect how you provide your services should be added to you philosophy as your reference service policies.

As an example, the reference desk in your library is very busy. It's so busy that you limit the amount of time you can spend helping any one person to five minutes. However, this is an unofficial policy. You bring someone in from another school to evaluate your reference service. This person notes that you don't give students much of your time and you rush from one person to the next. These comments lower your evaluation, but the evaluator was unaware of your reference practices. Eliminate the potential for misunderstandings and miscommunications by spelling out your reference policies. If your policies say that you cannot spend any more than five minutes helping any one patron, then you should get high marks if you adhere to this and low ones if you take too much time.

Remember that your reference policy is not carved in stone, and is subject to evaluation as well. If you find through the evaluation process that the goals outlined in your reference policies are unachievable, always achievable, or too vague to know if you are achieving them, then it is time to change your reference policies. The process of evaluation has given you the evidence you need to make an informed decision about and an appropriate change to your reference policies.

Guidelines for Performance

So you have a reference policy at your library. You feel it is a good one, and it accurately represents what you can do given your circumstances. Now, how do you judge how well you are doing it?

This is where having some kind of standard or guidelines will be a big help. We mentioned the RUSA guidelines for behavioral performance in Chapter 5. *Guidelines for Behavioral Performance of Reference and Information Service Providers* (2004; http://www.ala.org/ala/mgrps/divs/rusa/resources/guidelines/guidelinesbehavioral.cfm) lists five areas of performance. The five areas of performance outlined in the guidelines are

- Approachability
- Interest
- Listening/Inquiring
- Searching
- Follow-up

Guidelines like these are very important because they outline good and appropriate behaviors you should be using when dealing with your students and teachers. Our behavior is crucial to the success of the process. In a study by Gers and Seward (1985), they found that librarians showing the least interest in a question answered that question correctly only 33 percent of the time, while librarians showing the most interest in the question were likely to answer it correctly 76 percent of the time. Another study by Andaleeb and Simmonds (1998) found that the demeanor of the staff played an important role in the customer's satisfaction with the library. This really validates the significance of the *Behavioral Guidelines.*

The difference between a statement of purpose and performance guidelines is subtle, and you might think that we don't need to talk about both. However, together they will help you provide good reference service to your students and teachers. Your statement of purpose, your reference philosophy, will help you stay focused on the important things you are trying to do in your media center. Your guidelines will help you carry out those important things in more meaningful ways for your students and teachers. For example, if your statement of purpose gives definite priority to providing instruction, then when a student asks you a question while you are shelving a book you remember to give priority to the instruction first. Your guidelines will help you carry out that instruction in a good way for your students and teachers.

Everyone who is going to be evaluated by these guidelines must be very familiar with them. You or the evaluator needs to know these guidelines well. You obviously cannot evaluate staff with these guidelines if they have never heard of them. You cannot conduct evaluations based on these guidelines if you do know what they mean or how they apply to the reference transaction. Give everyone involved a copy of the guidelines and talk about them at that time. Make sure everyone understands that you will be evaluating their behavior based on these guidelines. Meet with everyone, again, after they have had time to get familiar with the guidelines, and ask if everyone understands them or has questions about them. Now you can talk about how you are going to carry out the evaluation process.

Why Evaluate?

Finally, before you get started, you need to know the answer to the question why are we evaluating? What is the purpose of going through this process?

The answer is often "to improve service." While this is a valid reason, how are you going to use the results of this process to improve service? Will you hold training sessions to address any deficiencies you find? Talk about this with your staff before beginning so they know what the outcome will be. However, if there is no follow through on the process—if you aren't going to use the results to improve service, then do not do it. You will make a lot of work for yourself and others, and you may offend or alienate your staff by making them participate in a meaningless exercise. Keep in mind though, that if you're not examining your service, then you don't necessarily know what you're doing poorly, or for that matter, what you're doing well.

Once you have done all your homework and preparation, then you are ready to evaluate!

HOW TO EVALUATE

There are two basic approaches to evaluating reference service.

- Evaluate reference desk staff
- Evaluate the user's satisfaction

These approaches are not mutually exclusive. You should do both. You don't have to do them both at the same time, but that is a possibility. Evaluation is a tricky process. It is important to evaluate not only how well you think you are doing things, but also how well others think you are doing things.

Evaluate the Librarian

There are two approaches to evaluating the librarian. You can conduct an unobtrusive study, or you can conduct—well—an obtrusive study. In an unobtrusive study, you recruit customers to ask a set of preselected questions of your staff without their knowing what the questions will be. You do want to tell your staff what you are doing and give them some general dates. You don't want evaluation to be a surprise. You don't want your staff to feel like you're spying on them with the intent of punishing mistakes.

A recent unobtrusive study of e-mail and chat reference services from public and academic libraries showed that these services achieved only a 55 percent success rate, which is the same number that in-person reference studies often find (Kaske and Arnold 2002). Like many of these studies, this study had to judge what was a right and wrong answer. The questions in the study were supposed to be representative of typical questions. All of the questions had two parts and most of them were difficult questions, which could explain the success rate. For example, one of the questions asked where and from what Chaucer died. The first part of this question is easy. Many reference sources list when and where people died, like *Almanac of Famous People*, but finding what Chaucer died from is beyond most reference sources. So if one of your staff got the first part of this question right, but not the second, would you say they answered correctly or incorrectly? This is one of the problems with an unobtrusive study. How do you pick good, representative questions and how do you score the answers to them? The best approach is to use variations of questions you've received and questions you develop from reading the literature of evaluation.

Another thing to think about with this method of evaluation is do you want the student who poses the question to also evaluate the librarian for their performance on the behavioral guidelines? That's a lot for a student to do. If you don't want them to do this, are you going to evaluate your staff's behavioral performance at all?

Unobtrusive evaluations work best in large environments with many employees and lots of business. The questions and the customers remain anonymous. In a small library, the questions may stand out and the unobtrusive evaluation becomes obvious. If there are only two of you, and you're conducting the evaluation, this method is obviously not going to work. In this case, try the method discussed below.

The opposite of the unobtrusive evaluation is to be obtrusive. Let's call it a collegial or peer evaluation. With this method, you perform the evaluation by sitting with your colleague at the reference desk. You listen to the questions they receive, the answers they give, and you watch the behaviors they exhibit in helping students. This method is much easier to implement. There is no development of representative questions. There is no need to recruit and train students to participate. There is no need to worry about how to evaluate behavior. You are right there to do it all.

When looking at the "rightness" of an answer, think about the resources—electronic or print—that were selected, the search statement used, and the process your colleague followed to find an answer. Ask whether that was or was not what you would have selected, your search statement, your process. Then ask if what they did was better, worse, or just different from what you would have done. At this point, you can make a judgment about the "rightness" of their answer. However, instead of splitting what may be some fine hairs concerning right and wrong, make a judgment about the quality of their overall search strategy. That fits nicely with the *Behavioral Guidelines*.

The problem with a peer evaluation is that your presence has an effect on your colleagues' behavior. You are not seeing them as students experience them. You are seeing them on their best behavior, putting forth their best effort. As long as you are aware of this influence, this approach can be extremely valuable. You presence may encourage your staff to be more aware of their behavior and its effects on the reference transaction when you're not around.

One problem with this method that you will encounter as you shadow your colleague around is refraining from answering questions yourself. It's hard to stand back, evaluating, and not jump in and help out, especially if the desk gets busy. It's OK to answer a few questions, but try to direct the business to the person being evaluated in order to have enough transactions to make the evaluation meaningful.

For any evaluation method, it is important to keep in mind that what a school media specialist is really trying to do is help the students and teachers become more information literate. You are not always just trying to give them the right answer but to help them find answers themselves, and all evaluations should be designed with that in mind. Remember, this should be reflected in your reference policy.

Evaluate User Satisfaction

The other method for evaluating reference service, and library service in general, is to survey the library's users. Some might say that what you are evaluating is not your service but how others *perceive* your service. Even if perception does not match reality, it is somebody's truth. Your teachers could believe that your library has outdated services and collections, even though you made a concerted effort to improve both, and this erroneous, negative perception is having a negative impact on your library. The way others perceive your service is important to any school media program. How can you be a leader and collaborate with others at your school if they perceive you as power hungry or territorial? Your school's perception of you is something you want to know about and improve on.

This type of survey can be done either as a general survey of satisfaction with library services, or as a follow-up survey to a reference transaction. It is difficult to get good information about reference transactions in a general survey that is passed out as users enter or leave the library. They may fill out the survey long after the reference transaction or they may not use reference services at all.

Using the follow-up survey is a good way to determine if the customer felt the transaction was a success or not. You, a colleague or a student can either hand out a survey after a reference transaction, or ask the student if they were satisfied with the service they received and record their answer. Nixon and Miller (2008) outline a simple, short survey to get feedback from both the librarian and the customer from a reference transaction that will give you an understanding of the perceived success of reference transactions in your library.

Perhaps the best approach is to use a combination of evaluation techniques. Do a general user satisfaction survey and a peer evaluation of reference service. Or do a peer evaluation and a follow-up question with the student who used the service. Pick and choose the things that you think will work best for your situation. Don't be afraid to call the whole process a trial, especially the first time you go through the process. Evaluate how it went with your staff. If you think you took the wrong approach, throw out the results, learn from the experience and do it better next time.

Below are two sample forms. Figure 13.1 is to be used by you and your staff as you evaluate each other. Record your impressions of behavioral performance in the first section. Make any comments about the behavior of the staff member being reviewed in the second section, and record questions, search strategies, and answers in the third section.

The second form, Figure 13.2, is for conducting a follow-up survey of students. You can hand these out right after a reference transaction and collect them in a box by the door. It gives the students a chance to record their satisfaction with the reference transaction in the boxes at the top of the form and make any comments about the service they received in the boxes at the bottom of the form.

WHAT IF IT'S ONLY YOU?

All this talk of evaluation is well and good, but what if you are the only person in the library/media center? What should you do then?

You can ask for outside help in evaluating your library, and your reference skills in particular. This can be problematic. You might be tempted to ask a teacher or principal to help you. Although it may prove that their opinions and

Figure 13.1. Reference Evaluation Form

Name: Date: Time: Place:

	Strongly Disagree	**Disagree**	**Undecided / Neutral**	**Agree**	**Strongly Agree**
Approachability					
Interest					
Listening / Inquiring					
Searching skills					
Follow-up					

Comments about behavioral performance:

Questions from users:

Figure 13.2. User Satisfaction Form

Name: Date: Time: Place:

User Satisfaction					
	Strongly Disagree	Disagree	Undecided/ Neutral	Agree	Strongly Agree
The answer I received was accurate and helpful.					
The service I received from the librarian was good.					

Comments from users:

perceptions are valuable to you, their input is at best incomplete. You probably do not want a non-librarian evaluating your library skills. Yes, they are fellow educators, but they are not librarians. They may not understand how library services function, and may not be capable of making informed judgments.

If you have a friend, colleague, or acquaintance who is a librarian, and she is willing to help you out, ask them. You want someone who will be fair and honest, but you also want someone who understands what librarians do and how they do it. If you can't think of anyone to help you with the evaluation process, call your nearest college or university library. Academic librarians generally like doing things like this. It is good community relations for them and makes them look good to their administration.

Evaluating yourself can be problematic. It is difficult to be fair and objective when it comes to your own performance. Some people will believe that they are better than they are, while others will be overly critical of their performance. In fact, it is even difficult to be aware of everything you're doing at the desk. However, writing a short self-assessment of your experiences at the reference desk, what you try to do and how well you think you do it, can be a good learning experience, like the reflection papers we assign our students.

Another thing you can do is pick out one of the behaviors from the *Behavioral Guidelines* and work on that while you're at the reference desk. For example, pick approachability. When you get to the desk, make an effort to be aware of everything you do that helps or hurts your approachability. Do you bring work to the desk? Do you look up often from that work? Do you walk around the library? Do you ask students if you could help them? Concentrate only on one of the five guidelines at a time. Next week, work on another one.

You can also keep track of the questions you had trouble answering. When you get some free time, go back to these questions and try them again, but take a different approach. Try different resources, different keywords, and different searches. Really try to find the answer. Whether you do or not, evaluate what you tried. If you found the answer, was it in a resource you were unaware of, or did you think about the question from a new perspective? If you didn't find the answer, is there a resource you don't have that might have helped, can you get help from someone else, or is there a good referral you could have given the student, or is there no good answer to the question?

Finally, you can survey the students. Before undertaking a survey, make sure to do research about other such projects first. This will help you put together a better survey. Remember that a user satisfaction survey will give you an important part of the picture of how well your library is performing, but it is only a part of the picture.

PUTTING IT ALL TOGETHER

So you've done a survey. You and your colleagues watched each other at the desk. You kept track of your reference transactions. You've got a lot of information that took a lot of effort to collect. What do you do with it? Write a report!

A report is a great way to get the word out about how well you are doing in the library and remind administrators of the important role the library plays in the successful education of students. Reports are useful because they force you to analyze and summarize the information you have collected. A report is also your and your institution's memory of special projects like an evaluation project. By collecting information regularly, you will be able to spot trends and identify strengths and weakness.

Sometimes you might not want to write a report because the information may not be flattering, but, in general, you should write the report anyhow. Pointing out your library's weaknesses to others may be just what you need to get help with a problem. A report of your activities will also show your strengths. That's a good thing! You are not often given the chance to tell everyone how good you and your staff are. A report is that chance. It will not lead to a big pay raise, but maybe you will get a pat on the back.

You should write a report every year that summarizes the library's activities throughout the past year. Since you no doubt have to pass statistics along to your principal and district, write your annual report at that time. Write reports about special projects at the time you complete the project so the information is fresh in your mind, then include a summary of that report in your annual report. A report gives you a record of what happened, and each year you can use the previous year's report as a template for your new report. Including statistics from previous years in your current report allows you to see and comment on trends. A report without analysis of the information presented is not worth doing because it will not mean anything to the person who reads it. So always explain what your statistics are, what they mean, and what trends you may be able to see by looking at them.

Here's an example. Let's say you included the number of reference transactions your library received in your report and it looked like this:

Current year	600
Past year	501
Two years ago	499

How do you explain your 20 percent increase when your enrollment has been static? You notice when examining your statistics that your instruction sessions have also increased by the same percentage. Now you can say that you believe the increase in reference questions is attributed to the increase in library instruction. But why did library instruction increase? Here you can mention that you worked closely with two teachers over the past year, helping them develop assignments with information literacy components and performing a number of library instruction sessions, and this successful experience has encouraged you to expand this service to all teachers in the coming year.

Finally, evaluation is a learning experience. You learn not only yours and your library's strengths and weaknesses, but you learn how to evaluate and improve the process of evaluation in the future. Evaluation results in an opportunity to improve your services and yourself. Writing a report allows you to record your experiences and share them with others. It preserves the knowledge you gained from the evaluation process, and gives you insight into what to examine closely the next time. Evaluation should be an integral process within your library. Without the opportunity to assess, evaluate, and analyze what you are doing, you will not understand the success or failure of your programs and services, and you will have missed an opportunity for growth.

Chapter 14

The Value of Your Reference Skills and Collection to Your School

In this chapter we'll look at some ways to share your knowledge and collections with your school, and we'll conclude by taking a brief look at the value of libraries to their schools.

JUST WHAT IS A REFERENCE COLLECTION THEN?

The discussions about the reference collection in the previous chapters may have led you to change your definition of just what a reference collection is. The reference collection includes more than the resource books on your shelves. Nowadays a good reference collection includes a variety of electronic sources and indexes of course, but even more than that, the reference section of any school media center includes human resources in the library and at your school, and, very specifically, you.

As the media specialist your knowledge and skills about teaching, learning, and technology as well as your attitudes and skills about sharing them to promote literacy all play an important part in the overall makeup of your reference collection. The reference skills and attitudes of the teachers and aides at your school, along with those of the students themselves, are all within your influence and can help to shape and define the basic reference collection and service at your media center. Thinking about our reference collections in this way paints a bigger picture of our reference services that is likely to lead to higher levels of information literacy throughout the whole school.

HOW DO YOU MEASURE HOW GOOD YOUR REFERENCE COLLECTION IS?

We have talked about a few ways to evaluate your reference collection and its services, but the best way to really measure a reference collection is by how well it gets used. You can have all the best books, train your staff and teachers perfectly, but if students don't end up using all the resources and services in meaningful ways, then your reference collection doesn't end up being very valuable at all.

When students use the reference collection and resources in meaningful ways, they will become more information literate, and naturally flow through the nine student information literacy standards and the standards for twenty-first century learners. Your reference collection will be busy as students use the resources to create projects, solve problems, and in other ways meet their curricular assignments and pursue interests. Teachers will visit with you regularly to collaboratively make decisions for their classes that take advantage of the resources in your reference collection and library, as well as your reference skills.

THREE CENTRAL IDEAS FOR PROMOTING THE BIG PICTURE OF THE REFERENCE COLLECTION

If all of this sounds a little idealistic, *Information Power* (1998) suggests three central ideas that media specialists should embrace in order to effectively promote information literacy in K-12 schools: Leadership, Collaboration, and Technology. We've provided suggestions on how school reference librarians can be good leaders and collaborators and use technologists to enhance literacy at their schools, but let's take one last look at these three important ideas as they relate to your references services.

Leadership

Leadership is having a vision you have shared with the teachers and administration at your school and convincing them to work with you toward that common goal. The goal we have regarding our reference collection is that we find ways to use all of our reference resources to promote information literacy at our school. Information literacy is the reason we buy books, provide access to databases, do library instruction and provide all our references services.

In order to be a leading influence at our schools in promoting literacy, media specialists should be involved in curriculum and reading committees of all kinds. This means more work of course, but how can you help to guide and influence learning and literacy if you are not involved at a design level with the basic literacy programs at your school?

Collaboration

In Chapter 11 we discussed the four legs of the metaphorical collaborative bench: maintain professional relationships, know the learning activities in each classroom, gather the best resources, and promote/teach those resources.

Implementing these four principles at your school will put you in a position to use the resources of your library on a daily basis to help teachers meet their existing curriculum goals better. It will also give you the opportunity to meet your own curricular goals and promote information literacy throughout your school, not in isolation, but within the context of preexisting assignments and activities. This is where you have the opportunity best to fulfill your role as a teacher and instructional partner through good collaboration.

Technology

In order to be a leader and a strong collaborator, you have a responsibility to stay current with information technologies as they relate to information literacy. How can you expect to provide suggestions or lead if you don't know what is available or how to use it effectively?

As a school media specialist, you have an obligation to be the expert at your school in current technologies, particularly those that will help promote information literacy.

So use your reference skills to find and read articles from the professional literature and explore training opportunities that will increase your awareness of new products, services, and trends. Try new software and evaluate it. Think about how you might be able to use it in the library or how your teachers might use it in the classroom. Will it enable you to do something new or add value to something you already do? Will it be easy to incorporate and learn? Will it be cost effective? If a colleague gets a new piece of hardware, take a field trip to see it. Ask what she bought it for and how she envisions using it. Will it work at your school? Will there be strong interest in using it?

VALUE

We have talked about ways you can demonstrate the value of your reference collection and services through collaboration, library instruction, chat reference, and many other tools. It is essential that you do these things to have a successful library media center. If you need help in convincing teachers and administrators to work with you, when your great example alone is not enough, then point to the research.

There are many research articles that prove the value of school libraries to education through higher student achievement on standardized test. A study of schools in Colorado (Lance, Rodney, and Hamilton-Pennell 2000) shows that CSAP reading test scores increase with increases in library media staff hours and expenditures. A similar study of Wisconsin schools (Smith 2006) echoes the same finding and adds that at the highest performing schools, library media specialists spent more time on instructional activities with teachers and students and more time on leadership activities like planning. In addition, school libraries with qualified school library media specialists have higher achievement than those without (Abram 2007). To see more of these state studies, go to the "School Library Impact Studies" page, which is part of the Library Research Services Web site (http://www.lrs.org/impact.php).

Studies have also been conducted on library instruction, just one aspect of all that we do. These studies show the positive impact of library instruction on student achievement (Eisenberg and Brown 1992). A fairly new field of study in library science is looking at the return on investment (ROI) of libraries. While there isn't an ROI study of school libraries yet, a study of Florida's public libraries (Monroe 2005) showed that for each dollar spent, the state received a benefit of $6.54. A similar study at the University of Illinois (Kaufman 2008) showed that for each dollar spent on the library, the university received $4.38 in grant income. When these studies reach school libraries, what will the ROI be? What do you think your school library's ROI will be?

What we do has value. The better we do it, the higher our students achieve. While resources play in important role, you are the most important ingredient to a successful school library media center. Your references services and skills are at the heart of your library and provide a strong foundation from which to lead, collaborate, and embrace changing technologies that will guide our schools into the information literacy of the future.

References

"2007 Encyclopædia Britannica." *Encyclopædia Britannica: Welcome Educators!*. http://info.eb.com/html/product_encyclopaedia_britannica.html (accessed December 23, 2008).

Abram, Stephen. "The Value of Our Libraries: Impact, Recognition and Influencing Funders." *Arkansas Libraries*. 64, no. 4 (Winter 2007): 5–11.

Alexander, Carter. "Co-Operation in Teaching Elementary-School Pupils to Use Library Materials." *The Elementary School Journal*. 39, no. 6 (February 1939): 452–459.

American Reference Books Annual. Englewood, CO: Libraries Unlimited, 2008.

Andaleeb, Syed Saad, and Patience L. Simmonds. "Explaining User Satisfaction with Academic Libraries: Strategic Implications." *College & Research Libraries*. 59 (1998): 156–167.

Anderson, Nate. "Using crowdsourced librarians to outsmart Google." *Ars Technica*, November 11, 2008. http://arstechnica.com/old/content/2008/11/using-crowdsourced-librarians-to-out-google-google.ars (accessed January 30, 2009).

Barker, Joe. "Best Search Tools Chart." *Infopeople: Moving Libraries Forward*, September 2, 2008. http://www.infopeople.org/search/chart.html (accessed January 30, 2009).

Bibel, Barbara. "Encyclopedia Update: 2008." *Booklist Online*, September 15, 2008. http://www.booklistonline.com/default.aspx?page=show_product&pid=2935134 (accessed December 23, 2008).

Breeding, Marshall. "lib-web-cats." *Library Technology Guides*, 2007. http://www.librarytechnology.org/libwebcats/ (accessed January 9, 2009).

Breeding, Marshall. "Major Open Source ILS Products." *Library Technology Reports*. 44, no. 8 (November 2008): 16–31.

Brunner, Borgna. "Everest Almanac: Adjusting to Everest's New Height." *Infoplease*, 2008. http://www.infoplease.com/spot/everest-height1.html (accessed May 5, 2009).

Casson, Lionel. *Libraries in the Ancient World*. New Haven, CT: Yale University, 2001.

"Catalog." *Merriam-Webster Online Dictionary*. http://www.merriam-webster.com/dictionary/catalog (accessed January 9, 2009).

Chan, Lois Mai. *Cataloging and Classification: An Introduction*. New York: McGraw-Hill, 1994.

Critical Thinking; Basic Theory and Instructional Structures. Wye Mills, MD: Foundation for Critical Thinking, 1997.

Eisenberg, Michael B., and Michael K. Brown. "Current Themes Regarding Library and Information Skills Instruction: Research Supporting and Research Lacking." *American Association of School Librarians*, Winter 1992. http://www.ala.org/ala/mgrps/divs/aasl/aaslpubsandjournals/slmrb/editorschoiceb/infopower/selecteisenberg.cfm (accessed May 4, 2009).

Eisenberg, Michael B., and Robert E. Berkowitz. *The Big6 in Secondary Schools*. Worthington, OH: Linworth, 2000.

"Encyclopedia." *Wikipedia, the free encyclopedia*, 2008. http://en.wikipedia.org/wiki/Encyclopedia (accessed December 19, 2008).

Fennell, Charles Augustus Maude, and John Frederick Stanford. "Encyclopaedia." *The Stanford Dictionary of Anglicised Words and Phrases*, 1892. http://books.google.com/books?id=0KAYAAAAIAAJ&printsec=titlepage&dq=The+Stanford+Dictionary+of+Anglicised+Words+and+Phrases#PPR13,M1 (accessed May 5, 2009).

"Frequently Asked Questions: Standards and Guidelines." *American Association of School Librarians*, 2008. http://www.ala.org/ala/mgrps/divs/aasl/aaslproftools/learningstandards/standardsfaq.cfm (accessed December 15, 2008).

Gers, Ralph and Lillie J. Seward. "Improving Reference Performance: Results of a Statewide Study." *Library Journal*. 110, no. 18 (1985): 32–35.

Gillispie, Charles Coulston. "Boole, George." *Dictionary of Scientific Biography*. New York: Scribner, 1970.

Gillispie, Charles Coulston. "Venn, John." *Dictionary of Scientific Biography*. New York: Scribner, 1970.

Grassian, Esther S., and Joan R. Kaplowitz. *Information Literacy Instruction: Theory and Practice*. New York: Neal-Schuman, 2001.

Gross, June, and Susan Kientz. "Collaborating for Authentic Learning." *Teacher Librarian*. 27, no. 1 (October 1999): 21.

Guide to Reference Books. 11th ed. Chicago: American Library Association, 1996.

"Guidelines for Behavioral Performance of Reference and Information Service Providers." *American Library Association*, June 2004. http://www.ala.org/ala/mgrps/divs/rusa/resources/guidelines/guidelinesbehavioral.cfm (accessed February 16, 2009).

Hernon, Peter, and Ellen Altman. *Assessing Service Quality: Satisfying the Expectations of Library Customers*. Chicago: American Library Association, 1998.

Hernon, Peter, and Charles R. McClure. "Unobtrusive Reference Testing: The 55 Percent Rule." *Library Journal*. 111, no. 7 (1986): 37–41.

Hubbertz, Andrew. "The Design and Interpretation of Unobtrusive Evaluations." *Reference & User Services Quarterly*. 44, no. 4 (Summer 2005): 327–335.

Hysell, Shannon Graff. *Recommended Reference Books for Small and Medium-sized Libraries and Media Centers: 2009 Edition, Volume 29*. 2009th ed. Libraries Unlimited, 2009.

"IFLA Digital Reference Guidelines." *International Federation of Library Associations and Institutions*, March 6, 2008. http://www.ifla.org/VII/s36/pubs/drg03.htm (accessed April 9, 2009).

"Information." *McGraw-Hill Dictionary of Scientific and Technical Terms*. 5th ed. 1994.

Information Power: Building Partnerships for Learning. Chicago: American Library Association, 1998.

Janssen, Sarah, ed. "Height of Mount Everest." *The World Almanac and Book of Facts, 2008*. 140th ed. New York, NY: World Almanac Books, 2008.

Kaske, Neal, and Julie Arnold. "An Unobtrusive Evaluation of Online Real Time Library Reference Services." Library Research Round Table, American Library Association, Annual Conference, Atlanta, Georgia, June 15, 2002.

Kaufman, Paula T. "The Library as Strategic Investment: Results of the Illinois Return on Investment Study." *Liber Quarterly: The Journal of European Research Libraries*. 18, no. 3/4 (December 2008): 424–436.

Lance, Keith Curry. "Impact of School Library Media Programs on Academic Achievement." *Teacher Librarian*. 29, no. 3 (February 2002): 29.

Lance, Keith Curry, Marcia J. Rodney, and Christine Hamilton-Pennell. *How School Librarians Help Kids Achieve Standards: The Second Colorado Study*, April, 2000. ERIC. http://www.eric.ed.gov/ERICWebPortal/contentdelivery/servlet/ERICServlet?accno=ED445698 (accessed May 4, 2009).

"Library Media." *Utah Education Network*. http://www.uen.org/core/librarymedia/index.shtml (accessed May 5, 2009).

Lorenzen, Michael. "A Brief History of Library Instruction in the United States of America." *LibraryInstruction.com*, 2003. http://www.libraryinstruction.com/lihistory.html (accessed March 26, 2009).

McBrien , J. Lynn, and Ronald S. Brandt. *The Language of Learning : A Guide to Education Terms*. Alexandria, VA: Association for Supervision and Curriculum Development, 1997.

"Merriam-Webster's Collegiate Dictionary, Eleventh Edition." *Merriam-Webster Online*. http://www.merriam-webster.com/cgi-bin/book.pl?c11.htm&1 (accessed November 3, 2008).

Monroe, Wanda. "Libraries Return on Investment Study." *Library Mosaics*. 16, no. 6 (December 2005): 12–13.

Murray, Janet. "Big6 Skills and State Standards." *The Big6*, January 30, 2003. http://www.big6.com/2003/01/30/big6-skills-and-state-standards/ (accessed May 5, 2009).

Niemeler, Kathy. "Telecom Primer." *Information Today*. 0, no. 0 (November 1983): 16–17.

Nixon, Judith M., and Jonathan Miller. "Quick and Easy Reference Evaluation: Gathering Users' and Providers' Perspectives." *Reference & User Services Quarterly*. 47, no. 3 (Spring, 2008): 218–222.

O'Gorman, Jack, ed. *Reference Sources for Small and Medium Sized Libraries*. 7th ed. American Library Association, 2007.

Osborne, Andrew. "Library Automation Systems and Vendors on the WWW," 2007. http://libinfo.com/vendors-systems.html (accessed January 9, 2009).

Papers and Proceedings of the Twenty-Ninth Annual Meeting of the American Library Association. Asheville, NC, 1907. http://books.google.com/books?id=kA8bAAAAMAAJ (accessed February 27, 2009).

"Presidential Committee on Information Literacy: Final Report." January 10, 1989. *Association of College and Research Libraries*. American Library Association. http://www.ala.org/ala/mgrps/divs/acrl/publications/whitepapers/presidential.cfm (accessed April 30, 2009).

Price, Anne. *Children's Catalog*. 19th ed. H. W. Wilson, 2006.

Price, Anne. *Middle And Junior High School Library Catalog*. 9th ed. H. W. Wilson, 2005.

Rethlefsen, Melissa L. "Easy ≠ Right." *Library Journal.* 133 (July 2, 2008): 12–14.

Richardson, Jr., John V. "Reference is Better Than We Thought." *Library Journal.* 127, no. 7 (2002): 41–42.

Salony, Mary F. "The History of Bibliographic Instruction: Changing Trends from Books to the Electronic World." *Reference Librarian.* 24, no. 51/52 (1995): 31.

Schneider, Karen G. "The Distributed Librarian: Live, Online, Real-Time Reference." *American Libraries.* 31, no. 10 (November 2000): 64.

"School Libraries." *ERIC—Education Resources Information Center.* http://www.eric.ed.gov/ERICWebPortal/Home.portal?_nfpb=true&portlet_thesaurus_1_actionOverride=%2Fcustom%2Fportlets%2Fthesaurus%2FgotoDetail&_windowLabel=portlet_thesaurus_1&portlet_thesaurus_1term=School+Libraries&portlet_thesaurus_1fromSearch=false&portlet_thesaurus_1pageNumber=1&_pageLabel=Thesaurus (accessed April 25, 2009).

Shera, Jesse H. *Introduction to Library Science.* Littleton, CO: Libraries Unlimited, 1976.

Smith, Ester G. *Student Learning Through Wisconsin School Library Media Centers: Library Media Specialist Survey Report*, January 2006. http://www.dpi.wi.gov/imt/pdf/finallmssurvey06.pdf (accessed May 4, 2009).

"Standards for the 21-Century Learner." *American Association of School Librarians*, 2007. http://www.ala.org/ala/mgrps/divs/aasl/aaslproftools/learningstandards/AASL_LearningStandards.pdf (accessed December 15, 2008).

Tenopir, Carol. "Rethinking Virtual Reference." *Library Journal.* 129, no. 18 (November 11, 2004): 34.

Ulrich's International Periodicals Directory 2007. 45th ed. New York: Bowker, 2006.

Webber, Sheila, and Bill Johnston. "Information Literacy: definitions and models," September 3, 2006. http://dis.shef.ac.uk/literacy/definitions.htm (accessed November 3, 2008).

Webster's New International Dictionary of the English Language. 2nd ed. Springfield, MA: Merriam, 1953.

"We knew the web was big . . ." *Official Google Blog*, July 25, 2008. http://googleblog.blogspot.com/2008/07/we-knew-web-was-big.html (accessed January 30, 2009).

"Wind Speed (Surface)." *Guinness World Records, 2008.* Guinness World Records, 2007.

Zink, Stephen D. *Computer Output Microform Library Catalog: A Survey.* 1977. ED 191501.

Index

About the Authors

SCOTT LANNING is associate professor of library media and head of reference at Southern Utah University, Cedar City, UT.

JOHN BRYNER is instructor in teacher education at Brigham Young University, Provo, UT, and is a Web site developer.